Macromedia® Shockwave™ for Director®

Macromedia® Shockwave™ for Director®

Jason Yeaman

Victoria Dawson

Hayden Books

Macromedia Shockwave for Director

©1996 Jason Yeaman and Victoria Dawson

All rights reserved. Printed in the United States of America. No part of this book may be used or reproduced in any form or by any means, or stored in a database or retrieval system, without prior written permission of the publisher except in the case of brief quotations embodied in critical articles and reviews. Making copies of any part of this book for any purpose other than your own personal use is a violation of United States copyright laws. For information, address Hayden Books, 201 W. 103rd Street, Indianapolis, Indiana 46290.

Library of Congress Catalog Number: 96-75191
ISBN: 1-56830-275-4

Copyright © 1996 Hayden Books

Printed in the United States of America 1 2 3 4 5 6 7 8 9 0

Warning and Disclaimer

This book is sold as is, without warranty of any kind, either expressed or implied. While every precaution has been taken in the preparation of this book, the authors and Hayden Books assume no responsibility for errors or omissions. Neither is any liability assumed for damages resulting from the use of the information or instructions contained herein. It is further stated that the publisher and authors are not responsible for any damage or loss to your data or your equipment that results directly or indirectly from your use of this book.

Trademark Acknowledgments

All terms mentioned in this book that are known to be trademarks or service marks have been appropriately capitalized. Hayden Books cannot attest to the accuracy of this information. Use of a term in this book should not be regarded as affecting the validity of any trademark or service mark. Shockwave is a trademark of Macromedia.

About the Authors

Jason A. Yeaman is the 3D/Multimedia Designer for Macromedia's Creative Services department and cocreator of the first Shockwave movies for the Macromedia Web site. He formally spent four years as Senior Technical Engineer with the Macromedia Technical department. Prior to joining Macromedia, he worked for the software division of Industrial Light and Magic and was an independent multimedia consultant for major corporations.

Victoria Dawson produces the award-winning Macromedia World Wide Web site and was cocreator of the first Shockwave movies for the Macromedia Web site and Vanguard Gallery featuring CNN, *USA Today*, Sony Music, MTV, and *Time* magazine among many others. She is a frequent speaker on Shockwave and the Web at industry events, such as the Macromedia International User Conference, Digital Hollywood, Web Innovation, and ArtTeco. Before getting completely hooked on the Internet, she was a Senior Designer in the Macromedia Creative Services department, responsible for multimedia and graphic design on the Showcase CD, product packaging, and other printed collateral. She also cofounded Blasthaus, the first gallery dedicated to technology and art, located in the multimedia "gulch" in San Francisco, California.

Acknowledgments

Jason Yeaman

This book would not have been possible without love and support from my wife, Rachel—thank you for your patience. Also thanks to my mother, Laurie, and the following close friends, who were neglected because of the book: Andrew Berry, Mari Jonassen, Carrie Myers, and Jason Gorski. I would also like to thank the following Macromedians for support and ideas: Miles Walsh, David Mendels, Bob Tartar, Eric Wittman, Mike Seery, Lee Allis, Pete Caban, Craig Goodman, Traci Dos Santos, and Sherry Flanders-Page. Finally, a very special thank you to my grandfather and grandmother who shaped my life in ways I'm just now learning to understand. And to Oliver Langan for introducing me to the Macintosh. Thank you all.

Victoria Dawson

A very special thanks to my parents, Cree and Sandra, for their love, support, and wisdom. A special thanks to my brother, Andrew, for his perspective and encouragement. A special thanks to William for his patience and support (and for introducing me to his MacPlus years ago). A special thanks to Bud Colligan and Miles Walsh for the opportunity to make this possible. To the "Real World" Shockwave Developers, who generously shared their deepest secrets with everyone. To the Macromedia Showcase CD team, whose wonderful graphics appear throughout the book. (To get a free Showcase CD, call 1-800-326-2128.) My friends and colleagues at Macromedia—Christine, Natalie, Peter, Fred, Rachel, Scott, and Dave, who kindly put up with my grumblings about how tired I was from writing all night. And all my other friends who eventually gave up on me having a real life until this was finished.

Credits

Publisher
Lyn Blake

Managing Editor
Lisa Wilson

Acquisitions Manager
Karen Whitehouse

Development Editor
Marta Partington

Associate Marketing Manager
Meshell Dinn

Publishing Coordinator
Rosemary Lewis

Cover Designer
Aren Howell

Book Designer
Gary Adair

Production Team Supervisor
Laurie Casey

Production Team
Angela Calvert, Kim Cofer, Tricia Flodder, Joe Millay, Erich J. Richter, Scott Tullis, Christine Tyner, Karen Walsh

Indexer
Brad Herriman

Hayden Books

The staff of Hayden Books is committed to bringing you the best computer books. What our readers think of Hayden is important to our ability to serve our customers. If you have any comments, no matter how great or how small, we'd appreciate you taking the time to send us a note.

You can reach Hayden Books at the following:

Hayden Books
201 West 103rd Street
Indianapolis, IN 46290
(800) 428-5331 voice
(800) 448-3804 fax

Email addresses:

America Online: Hayden Bks
Internet: hayden@hayden.com

Visit the Hayden Books Web site at
http://www.hayden.com

Contents at a Glance

1	What Is Shockwave for Director?	1
2	Top Ways to Use Shockwave	9
3	Authoring Mulitmedia with Shockwave	25
4	New Director Authoring Techniques for Shockwave	37
5	Lingo Commands for Shockwave	57
6	Using Afterburner—Post Processor for Director	75
7	Adding Multimedia to Your Web Site	81
8	Shockwave and Your Web Server	93
9	Tips and Techniques from Real-World Shockwave Developers	101
10	The Next Wave—Shockwave 2.0	157
11	Shockwave for FreeHand	165
	Glossary	169
	Index	173

Table of Contents

1 What Is Shockwave for Director? 1
    Multimedia on the Internet 1
    Shockwave Versus Java 3
    Shockwave Essentials 5
    Shockwave Today and Tomorrow 5
        Macromedia Teams with Netscape to Lead the Way 6
        Future Shockwave-Compatible Browsers 7
2 Top Ways to Use Shockwave 9
    Multimedia Brings the Internet to Life 9
    The Top Ways to Use Shockwave 11
        High Impact Interfaces & Consumer Titles 13
        Online Advertising & Product Demonstrations 15
        Home Page Animations & Site Bytes 17
        Corporate Presentations 19
        Interactive Games & Virtual Worlds 21
        Educational Training & Tutorials 23
3 Authoring Multimedia with Shockwave 25
    Authoring Ideas 25
        Art with Director Effects and Transitions 26
        Re-Create Your Original Artwork 26
        Animated Small Buttons 26
        Make Lingo Movies 26
        The Basic Requirements 26
        Hardware for Authoring 33
    Understanding Download Times for Users 33
        Download Table 33
        Determining File Size 34
4 New Director Authoring Techniques for Shockwave 37
    Image Tips 37
        Thinking Small 38
        Cast Member Dithering 39
        Special 1-Bit Techniques 41
        Cropping Unused Color and Text 43
    Audio Techniques 44
        Audio Downsampling Techniques 44

Contents

- Audio Looping Techniques 47
- Turning Sound On/Off in Movies 48
- Cast and Score Tips 49
  - Ink and Transition Techniques 50
  - Movie Control Techniques 51
  - Cast Conservation Techniques 52
- Saving and Compressing Techniques 53

5 Lingo Commands for Shockwave 57

- New Shockwave Lingo Commands 57
  - GoToNetPage (URI) 58
  - GoToNetMovie (URI) 58
  - GetNetText (URI) 59
  - PreLoadNetThing (URI) 59
  - NetDone () 60
  - NetError () 61
  - NetTextResult () 61
  - NetMime () 62
  - NetLastModDate() 62
  - NetAbort 63
  - GetLatestNetID () 63
- Additional Lingo Examples and Ideas 64
  - The Time Command 64
  - The Date Command 64
  - Random HTTP Jumper 65
  - ColorDepth Control 65
  - SoundLevel Control 65
  - Custom Cursor in a Browser 66
  - Color 1-Bit Cast Members 67
  - Tracking User Input 67
- Disabled XObjects in Shockwave 68
  - 1. FileIO XObject 68
  - 2. SerialPort XObject 68
  - 3. OrthoPlay XObject 68
- Disabled Director-Related Commands 68
  - 1. Resource and XLib Commands 69
  - 2. Open Window and Close Window Commands 69
  - 3. ImportFileInto Command 69
  - 4. SaveMovie Command 70
  - 5. PrintFrom Command 70

	Disabled System-Related Commands 70
	1. Open 70
	2. Quit, Restart, and Shutdown Commands 71
	3. File Name, Path Properties, and Functions 71
	4. MCI Command 71
6	Using Afterburner—Post Processor for Director 75
	Optimal Compression Techniques for "Burning" Your Movies 75
	Current Compression 77
	Customized Compression Techniques 78
7	Adding Multimedia to Your Web Site 81
	"Smart" HTML Authoring for Shockwave 81
	Overall Page Sizes and Download Times 83
	Multiple Movies on a Page 84
	Sounds in Multiple Movies 84
	Looping Movies 84
	Writing HTML for Shockwave 84
	Netscape 2.0 Browser 85
	HTML for Netscape 2.0 86
	HTML for All Other Browsers 87
8	Shockwave and Your Web Server 93
	Uploading Your Files Properly 93
	File Transfer Protocol 94
	Binary Raw Data 94
	Setting Mime Types on Your Server 96
	UNIX Servers 96
	Mac HTTP Servers 97
	WebSTAR Server 97
9	Tips and Techniques from Real-World Shockwave Developers 101
	2-Lane Media 102
	About 2-Lane Media 102
	Company Focus 102
	Clients and Projects 103
	Impact of the Internet 103
	Why Shockwave? 103
	Shockwave Opportunities 104
	Your Ideal Future on the Internet with Shockwave 104
	Project One: "Panic in the Park" for Warner*Active* 104
	Project Two: The Fit Model for "The Spot" Web Site 109

Contents

CL!CK Active Media 112
    About CL!CK Active Media 113
    Company Focus 113
    Clients and Projects 113
    Impact of the Internet 113
    Why Shockwave? 113
    Shockwave Opportunities 114
    Your Ideal Future on the Internet with Shockwave 114
    Project: Dream a Dolphin's New Media
        Internship Competition 114

DAVIDEO 119
    About DAVIDEO 119
    Company Focus 119
    Clients and Projects 120
    Impact of the Internet 120
    Why Shockwave? 120
    Shockwave Opportunities 120
    Your Ideal Future on the Internet with Shockwave 121
    Project: Algorithmic Animations in Shockwave 121

Hands of Time 127
    About Hands of Time Animation & Design 128
    Company Focus 128
    Clients and Projects 129
    Professional Recognition 130
    Impact of the Internet 130
    Why Shockwave? 130
    Shockwave Opportunities 131
    Your Ideal Future on the Internet with Shockwave 131
    Project: Satan's 666 Pack Animations 132

M/B Interactive 136
    About M/B Interactive 137
    Company Focus 137
    Clients and Projects 137
    Impact of the Internet 138
    Why Shockwave? 138
    Shockwave Opportunities 138
    Your Ideal Future on the Internet with Shockwave 139

NewOrder Media 143
    About NewOrder Media 144
    Company Focus 144
    Clients and Projects 144

Impact of the Internet	144
Why Shockwave?	145
Shockwave Opportunities	145
Your Ideal Future on the Internet with Shockwave	146
Project: Shockwave, the Motion Picture for NewOrder Media	146
Saturday!	149
About Saturday!	149
Company Focus	149
Clients and Projects	150
Impact of the Internet	150
Why Shockwave?	150
Shockwave Opportunities	150
Your Ideal Future on the Internet with Shockwave	150
Project: Arcade Games in Shockwave	151
10 The Next Wave—Shockwave 2.0	157
Future Possibilities for Shockwave and the Internet	157
Data Transmission for Shockwave	160
11 Shockwave for FreeHand	165
How Is This Related to Shockwave for Director?	165
What Can I Put on the Web with FreeHand?	166
How Does It Work?	166
When Will Shockwave for FreeHand Be Available?	167
Future Applications	167
Glossary	169
Index	173

Foreword

Macromedia Brings Multimedia to World Wide Web

Millions of Netscape Navigator 2.0 users can now experience multimedia in a Web page and the dynamic impact of multimedia documents for the first time. Shockwave for Director brings Director productions with interactive graphics, sound, and animation to the Internet. Web developers are using Shockwave now for interactive entertainment, merchandising, advertising, product demonstrations, and education.

More than 300,000 creative professionals who already use Director are now able to transform static Web pages into compelling interactive advertising, promotions, entertainment, and educational experiences. The Shockwave technology has been adopted by Microsoft, Netscape, Navisoft, Sun Microsystems, CompuServe, and Silicon Graphics for integration into their Internet browsers, authoring tools, and/or related products. Using Netscape Navigator 2.0 and other popular browsers in the near future, users can download Director multimedia movies as quickly as a simple digitized image. Because Director is embedded into these browsers and/or tools, Director movies run seamlessly at full power on the user's local desktop. Therefore, only the movie content needs to be placed in Web pages for downloading.

Before Shockwave for Director, World Wide Web pages were limited to text and static graphics where small sound and video files had to be downloaded and played with shareware. With Shockwave for Director, millions of Internet users will now be able to experience multimedia in a Web page and the dynamic effect of multimedia documents. Because the Director multimedia playback engine can be easily installed into Netscape Navigator, it is completely transparent to the user. As the bandwidth of the Internet continues to expand with such breakthroughs as cable modems, complete multimedia titles created with Director will be seamlessly delivered over the Internet, making it an outlet for mainstream multimedia title distribution.

At the Shockwave launch in December 1995, Web publishers who unveiled new media content included a Who's Who of the Internet and multimedia worlds: CNN Online, Time Pathfinder, CondeNet Online, 20th Century Fox, MTV Online, Turner Online, Apple Computer, Disney's Toy Story, Intel, USA Today, Advertising Age, M/B Interactive, Sony Music Entertainment, Melrose Place, Internet Shopping Network, American Cancer Society, @Home, On Ramp, c|net online, Clement Mok Designs, Radical Media, Siegel & Gale, ad*hoc Interactive, and Maytag.

We hope you'll enjoy learning more about Shockwave for Director and that you'll SHOCK your Web site right away! Make sure that you check out all the latest shocked sites at the Shockwave Epicenter at www.macromedia.com.

Sincerely,

Bud Colligan

Bud Colligan
President & CEO
Macromedia

Introduction

With all the incredible hype surrounding the Internet today, it's often hard to keep track of fact versus fantasy. The World Wide Web is blazing ahead on the information superhighway—with record publicity surrounding everything from its phenomenal growth to the hottest content to the latest Web browsers.

One advancement certain to change the way the Web is created and used is Shockwave for Director, which brings high impact interactive multimedia to the Internet. Finally, true multimedia—incorporating graphics, sound, animations, text, 3D, and interactivity—can be brought instantly to Web users around the world. So where does a Web designer turn to figure out how to stay on the cutting edge? This book is a beginning—it's designed to get you started quickly with Shockwave.

Macromedia Shockwave for Director is a comprehensive guide that contains all the facts and techniques you need to know to work with Shockwave for Director. And because it's written completely from our viewpoint from the "inside" (and with over seven combined years of experience at Macromedia), we leave no stone unturned!

About This Book

Throughout this book you will find "The Insider's Perspectives" and "Macromedia Developer Profiles" that take you behind the corporate curtain and give the inside story on how Shockwave for Director was *really* developed over the last year. You'll get inside the Shockwave team's collective mind-set and before you know it, you'll be ready to "fry" your very own Director movies! You see, exploring all the angles of Shockwave and the Web is our job. We work right in the thick of it every day—Victoria as the Macromedia Web producer and Jason as a Director designer focusing on Shockwave and Internet playback.

We have been on this crazy roller coaster called Shockwave since its inception and now we'll be your tour guides. We hope you'll enjoy the ride as much as we do!

We have organized this book as a step-by-step process to get you started putting your multimedia on the Internet as quickly as possible so that you can use Shockwave effectively and efficiently. The process begins with a brief overview of Shockwave (see Chapter 1) and its top uses (see Chapter 2), authoring in multimedia (see Chapter 3), Internet authoring techniques (see Chapter 4), continuing on through advanced Lingo authoring techniques (see Chapter 5), compressing with Afterburner (see Chapter 6), the new HTML tags needed for Shockwave files (see Chapter 7), configuring your server for Shockwave (see Chapter 8), real-world tips (see Chapter 9), the future of Shockwave for Director and multimedia on the Internet (see Chapter 10), and the new Macromedia Shockwave technologies for FreeHand and Authorware (see Chapter 11).

Many of the skills and techniques explained in this book are also found on the *Macromedia Shockwave for Director* CD-ROM in a tutorial format so that you can follow along with the steps in the book at your own pace.

Who Needs to Read This Book

Anyone interested in adding multimedia to his or her Web site and who has a basic knowledge of the Web, Macromedia Director, and HTML can use this book to learn the basic and advanced principles of multimedia on the Internet and push the cutting edge of Web site design into the future. For the reader, it is important to understand the basics of Multimedia 101, such as the difference between the roles of programmer, graphic designer, wordsmith, and information designer. We expect this book to appeal to a great many computer literate Webmistresses and masters, HTML designers, multimedia developers, and everyday folk who want to explore interactive multimedia and the Internet simultaneously.

Getting Started with Shockwave

Before you begin to create Shockwave for Director files, you will need to have Macromedia Director software installed on your Windows or Macintosh system. For information about ordering Macromedia Director, call 1-800-326-2128; for upgrades to the latest Macromedia Director version, call 1-800-457-1774.

Also on the *Macromedia Shockwave for Director* CD-ROM, you will find a demo version of Macromedia Director to help you work through the tutorials on the CD. If, however, you want to create finished Shockwave movies of your own, you will need the commercial version of Macromedia Director.

The most recent Macromedia Shockwave Developer's Kit, which includes Afterburner and the Shockwave Plug-In for Internet browser for Windows and Macintosh, can be downloaded free from the Macromedia Web site at http://www.macromedia.com/.

Web Terms at a Glance

The World Wide Web, better know as the "Wild, Wild Web" in some cases, is the first true multimedia medium for the masses, yet full of obscure and often uncharted acronyms. With its rapid developmental pace, it is critical to stay "in the know" and keep up with the latest jargon. So here are some basic vocabulary terms you will need to understand before adding multimedia to your Web site. (For more extensive information, see the Glossary in the back of the book.)

HTML (HyperText Markup Language)

HTML is the standard international Web authoring language used for publishing text, graphics, and multimedia content on Web pages. To write HTML, one only needs a simple text editor or word processor for editing. If you want to learn more about HTML or create your own Web site, you can go to one of the many sites on the Web that offer free HTML instruction, because the Web itself houses thousands of pages on this subject. For more details, you can browse the Internet or your local bookstore for information. Here is an HTML sample from Macromedia's home page:

```
<html><head>
<title>Welcome to Macromedia!</title></head>
<body bgcolor="#000000" text="#ffffff" link="#00FFFF" vlink="#FF0000"> <p>

<H3 align=center>Welcome to the cutting edge of multimedia and design on the
web!</H3>

<p align=center> <a href="/Tools/Shockwave/index.html"><img border=0 src="Images/
shockhome.banner.gif" alt="Macromedia Shockwave for Director is Here!"></a>

<p align=center> <a href="Randmaps/spot5.map"><IMG border=0 SRC="Randmaps/
➥spot5.gif" ALT=""
ISMAP></a>

<P><center>
<a href="/Images/homepage.bar.map"><img ISMAP border=0 src="Images/
➥homepage.bar.gif" alt=""></a>
</center> <p>
Site last updated - <meta last_updated>02/13/96 08:38 AM PST
</center>

</body></html>
```

URL (Uniform Resource Locator)

An URL is the standard address for anything on the Internet. An example of an URL could be http://www.birthday.com/january/index.html. An URL has three specific parts:

- The Internet protocol (for example, http, ftp, gopher)
- The Internet host (for example, www.birthday.com)
- The hierarchy of directories and filenames (for example, january or index.html)

HTTP Server (HyperText Transport Protocol)

An HTTP server is a computer that delivers World Wide Web data across the Internet. It is predominantly based on UNIX machines. In response to a request for a specific URL, the HTTP server returns a block of data, plus the type of that data, or MIME type.

MIME Type (Multi-Purpose Internet Mail Extensions)

MIME type is a specification of the type of a block of data. In the context of the Web, MIME types specify which type of data is returned from a server.

MIME types can include the following:

- Text
- Graphics of various types (GIF or JPEG)
- Sound (WAV or AIF)
- Director movies (DCR, DIR, or DXR)

A MIME type consists of two parts: the content type and the content subtype.

DIR, DCR, and DXR (Shockwave for Director File Extensions)

Shockwave introduces three new Director and Afterburner file extensions for the Internet. Movies compressed through Afterburner use a DCR extension to identify them.

Regular uncompressed Director movies use a DIR extension and "protected" Director files use a DXR extension. The Shockwave Plug-In for Director recognizes Director or Afterburner movies with DCR, DIR, or DXR file extensions.

Hardware Requirements

We recommend that you use a standard IBM-compatible PC (386 or faster), a Power Macintosh (601 or faster), or a Macintosh (68030 or faster) configuration with at least 8 MB of RAM, 14.4 modem (or faster), a large hard drive, CD-ROM drive (2x or faster), Internet access from a local service provider, 16-bit sound card, and a large 256-color monitor.

Software Requirements

We recommend that you have the latest operating systems for your machine. For PCs, this is Windows 95 or Windows 3.1. and for the Macintosh, this is System 7 or later. We also recommend that you have an understanding of the basic principles of HTML editing, Macromedia Director, and an Internet browser like Netscape Navigator 2.0.

The Ever-Changing Industry

As we were finishing writing this book, new announcements from leading players in the industry, like Microsoft, Netscape, and Sun, were blitzing us on a daily basis. At the current rate, we knew we would never be finished writing, so that is why we created a home page for *Macromedia Shockwave for Director:* (`http://www.macromedia.com/Brain/Books/Hayden/Shockwave/`). You can visit this page for the latest resources including the Shockwave Plug-Ins, the latest version of Afterburner, general Web authoring information, *Macromedia Shockwave for Director* updates, and the latest on what's happening in the industry. We wanted to write a book that would provide a strong foundation for adding interactive multimedia to your Web pages with Shockwave for Director today *and* give you a springboard into what is yet to come on the Web. Master the principles outlined in this book and regardless of the future directions, you will be on the cutting edge with Shockwave for Director!

Meet the Shockwave Team

And now a word from the team that brought you indoor plumbing, sliced bread, and now Shockwave for Director! You'll be hearing their insights from ground zero during the Shockwave development cycle throughout the book, but now let's find out: Who are these caped crusaders?

Name: Bruce Hunt
Title: Director of Networked Players

Now tell us what you really do:

Find resources for the Shockwave Engineering and QA Team! Make sure that the Shockwave team makes and meets commitments. Collect features for future versions of Shockwave for Director. Plan feature roll-out in future version of Shockwave. My role is to draw the best out of the Shockwave Team.

One interesting fact about your job:

I always seem to be late for the train!

Name: Harry Chesley
Title: Senior Architect

Now tell us what you really do:

I program computers.

One interesting fact about your job:

I've been coding for over 25 years now, and I still do it for fun.

Name: Chris Walcott
Title: QA Entomologist & Drum Master

Now tell us what you really do:

I lead the Shockwave bug finding effort.

One interesting fact about your job:

I get to work with the coolest people in the computer industry.

Name: Sarah Allen
Title: "i write code"

Now tell us what you really do:

Mostly I've worked on getting Shockwave to play on the Mac. I've done some design, written some code, done lots of debugging, and fixed many bugs.

Introduction

One interesting fact about your job:

I don't have to wear shoes in the office.

Name: John Newlin
Title: I don't need no stinkin' title.

(One thing that I really like about Macromedia is that we are not tagged with titles. Well, there are some people here who enjoy having a big title, like Senior this or Senior that. But I prefer not having a title.... I enjoy the work that I do, and when I don't enjoy it anymore, I'll find someplace else to work...;)

Now tell us what you really do:

I'm the guy who took Director and made the playback engine work as a "pluggable" module under Windows. What this means is that we can plug it into Authorware, Netscape, and other browsers like Internet Explorer. I also track down and fix bugs associated with running as an embedded piece of software. I also worked on the Mac side of things back before Shockwave began.

One interesting fact about your job:

Just watching how fast things change on the Internet.

Name: Sherri Sheridan
Title: Shockwave Artist/Engineer

Now tell us what you really do:

Live, sleep, eat, and dream Shockwave.

One interesting fact about your job:

It never stops.

Name: Ken Day
Title: Senior Architect

Now tell us what you really do:

So for Shockwave, it was natural for me to take on the problem of optimizing the internal structures for Internet delivery. Really. And it's interesting, too. Can I show you my pocket protector? (Actually, I don't have one. I prefer the down-home look of ink stains on my jeans.) The other thing I do is whatever-it-takes-to-ship-this-damn-thing. A new dialog box? No problem. Some obscure sequence of animation and mouse clicks makes the machine roll over on its side and smoke? Time to dive in.

One interesting fact about your job:

What? :-) Oh... it must be interesting. It's pretty hard to describe the abstract beauty of a 3-D model of a computer problem that you toy with and mold until it's a solution.... What's surprising is that with my business-oriented database background, I've been able to make a contribution to an artistically oriented multimedia project. Joining this team was a major turning point in my career. What's easy to make interesting is the combination of people I work with—Harry, John, and I are pretty typical engineers. Sarah is the cross-over, both a solid programmer and an artist. Sherri and Chris are both primarily artists—Chris a musician and Sherri a multimedia artist. Toss in all the multifaceted people around us at Macromedia, and you've got an amazing brew. And we make a great team! Benefits of diversity? Amen.

Chapter 1

What Is Shockwave for Director?

If you are like most Director users, you are anxious to get started adding multimedia to your Web site immediately. This section will give you a brief overview of Macromedia Shockwave for Director, including the benefits it provides to the Internet industry, the software components it embodies, and the Internet browsers that support Shockwave's multimedia technology. With this information at your fingertips, you'll quickly see why Shockwave is changing the face of the Web forever.

Multimedia on the Internet

When the World Wide Web first started, Web pages were limited to text and static graphics. Small sound and video files were possible but only in a limited capacity. They had to be downloaded and individually played with shareware. Now, however, with the advent of

Shockwave for Director, millions of Internet users can experience the dynamic effects of a Web page that seamlessly incorporates interactive multimedia.

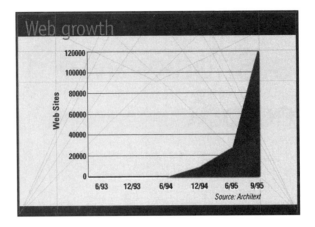

Macromedia's Shockwave brings the most innovative communication medium—multimedia—to today's fastest growing communication channel—the Internet. Shockwave for Director brings together the world of high impact graphics, sound, animations, text, and 3D with the Web and creates a revolutionary Internet browsing experience. Shockwave viewing functionality is currently available on the Netscape Navigator 2.0 browser for Windows and Macintosh and will soon be available for other browsers, including NaviSoft, Silicon Graphics WebForce, and CompuServe among other possible browsers, like the Microsoft Internet Explorer.

As the bandwidth of the Internet continues to expand with the help of breakthrough advances in cable modems and fiber optics, complete multimedia titles created with

Director will one day stream over the Internet, making it an outlet for mainstream multimedia title distribution as well as other bandwidth intensive files.

Shockwave for Director is based on the industry standard multimedia authoring tool, Macromedia Director. Today, over 300,000 developers are creating interactive multimedia using Director on Windows and Macintosh computers resulting in thousands of consumer CD-ROM titles, corporate presentations, interactive training, multimedia kiosks, and education courseware. The industry acceptance and authoring versatility of Director make it the natural foundation for Shockwave. But fortunately, you don't have to be an experienced computer programmer to author with Shockwave. Shockwave is simple and easy to learn. From beginner to expert computer users, everyone has the opportunity to make his or her Web sites interactive and engaging with Shockwave. This vast pool of creative talent is jump-starting a new era of multimedia on the Internet.

Shockwave Versus Java

Although at first glance Macromedia's Shockwave for Director and Sun Microsystems' Java may seem similar, they are different approaches to multimedia and appeal to very distinct users. Director is a multimedia authoring application that uses Lingo, a HyperTalk-like scripting language, while Java is an advanced programming language similar to C++. Shockwave for Director and Macromedia Director are optimized for creative professionals with little or no computer programming experience (graphic designers, desktop publishers, 3D artists, animators, sound specialists, digital imaging professionals, writers, corporate trainers, and educators). Java appeals primarily to computer programmer and engineer audiences who want to create secure, multiplatform, distributed applications and systems in the C++ programming language syntax.

Macromedia Shockwave for Director

Another significant difference between the two authoring tools involves the platforms on which they run. Director runs on Windows 3.1, Windows 95, Power Macintosh, and Macintosh. Director playback is available on the Internet, Windows 3.1, Windows 95, Power Macintosh, Macintosh, 3DO, OS/2, David, and other players that are planned to ship in the next six to nine months. The Java programming language is available from Sun in beta form on Solaris and Windows 95. Versions have been announced but are not available yet for Power Macintosh and Windows 3.1.

The Insider's Perspective

How do you see Shockwave and Java working together?

Bruce Hunt: Java is a platform-independent programming language. Shockwave is a tool for multimedia creation. Shockwave will be used by graphic artists and multimedia developers. Java will be used to create future versions of Shockwave. Part of Shockwave is a programming language called Lingo. It is designed to optimize the use of multimedia components. Java might be a great implementation language for Lingo.

Harry Chesley: That's like asking, "How do you see Director and C working together?" In many ways.

Chris Walcott: I see Java working in the background accessing databases and running applications. Shockwave is better at delivering content.

Sarah Allen: As soon as we ship Shockwave 1.0, I'll start thinking about that.

John Newlin: Interesting question. I think that Java will be the "glue" on the page that lets different HTML controls communicate with Shockwave movies. Java could also allow different Shockwave movies to communicate with each other on the same page. There are other things happening in this area that I can't talk about right now.

Sherri Sheridan: As an artist I'm not that interested in Java.

What Is Shockwave for Director?

Ken Day: Director is great for rapid development of rich multimedia productions. Java is great for development of complex, performance-sensitive new interactions. I expect to see Java applets used within Director titles. A few applications will need to be developed from the ground up in Java to get it completely right. But those will be high-budget affairs.

Shockwave Essentials

There are three essential components you need to get started creating your own multimedia Web pages: Macromedia Director, Afterburner, and the Shockwave Plug-In for your Shockwave-compatible browser:

- Macromedia Director is the industry-standard animation and authoring tool for multimedia production.
- Macromedia Afterburner is a post processor compression utility that compresses your Director files by approximately 60 percent, keeping their sizes small for optimal download times. As a result, some Shockwave files may be smaller than the original static graphics used in most Web sites today.
- Macromedia Shockwave Plug-In is the playback engine for files created using Macromedia's Director software. The Plug-In is integrated into a compatible browser, like Netscape Navigator, and is completely transparent to the user. This technology enables multimedia files authored on Windows or Macintosh computers to play back on the Internet instantly.

Shockwave Today and Tomorrow

Today Shockwave offers a wealth of new interactive experiences for the Internet surfer. It also creates new opportunities for the Web authors to express their content in Shockwave's media-rich environment. Some of these opportunities include innovative advertising, global presentations, home page animations, and interactive games. Shockwave's new method for high impact content delivery enables developers to reach new markets such as advertising and education through these immersive experiences.

Tomorrow's Shockwave will be affected by many factors ranging from radical improvements in the speed of our communications to new software improvements in Macromedia Director and Shockwave-compatible browsers. With future support for streaming and caching movies, Shockwave for Director sets a new level of interactive performance. See Chapter 10, "The Next Wave—Shockwave 2.0," for more information about Shockwave's future development.

Macromedia Teams with Netscape to Lead the Way

Macromedia and Netscape Communications started out on June 5, 1995 to create a technology integration that would change the character of the Web from static pages to dynamic, interactive multimedia. By integrating Macromedia's Director multimedia playback software into the Netscape Navigator browser software, they have both been successful.

What Is Shockwave for Director?

This combination of Netscape Navigator 2.0 and Macromedia's Shockwave for Director technology greatly expands the capabilities for communicating over the Internet by providing users with richer media and more compelling means of expression.

Macromedia's player technology enables developers to "Author Once, Play Anywhere," meaning they have the benefit of authoring titles on their development platform of choice, whether Windows or Macintosh, and then being able to deliver the titles on the most popular platforms in the industry, such as Windows, Macintosh, SGI, 3DO, OS/2, David, and now, the Internet.

Future Shockwave-Compatible Browsers

Shockwave technology has been officially adopted by NaviSoft, CompuServe, and Silicon Graphics for integration into their Internet browsers. The Microsoft Internet Explorer browser, among others, is also a likely candidate. Soon users of these browser can experience Director multimedia movies as quickly as a simple digitized image, just as in Netscape Navigator 2.0. Because the Shockwave Plug-In will function identically in each instance, only one Shockwave movie file needs to be placed in Web pages, part of the Shockwave "author once, play anywhere" philosophy.

The Insider's Perspective

Why call this technology "Shockwave"?

Bruce Hunt: Shockwave was the code name.

Harry Chesley: Shockwave is taken from the title of John Brunner's 1975 novel *The Shockwave Rider*, which, in turn, is based on the book *Future Shock* by Toffler.

Sarah Allen: Shockwave was the code name.

John Newlin: Harry named it Shockwave because he thought it would have ripple effects throughout the industry. I guess this book is evidence of that. :-)

Sherri Sheridan: Harry thought of it from the book *The Shockwave Rider*. I tried reading it, but it was too boring.

Ken Day: Shockwave was the code name. Marketing made the classic "mistake" of telling customers our internal code name, it got in the press, and we were stuck with it as a product name. Harry can tell you what went on in his head—it was a cool idea.

What would you have rather named it?

BH: Distributor (á la Director)

HC: I wouldn't change the name.

SA: I like the name.

JN: Stress Inducer :-)

SS: I love the name—it's perfect.

KD: Shockwave!

Chapter 2
Top Ways to Use Shockwave

Multimedia Brings the Internet to Life

Shockwave has created a revolution in the world of communication never before experienced on the Internet—suddenly the Internet is alive with vivid, full-motion animations, interactivity, and sound—creating unique experiences your users will never forget. Now more like television than a print medium, the Web is dynamic, interactive, and most importantly, has what it takes to dazzle consumers and keep them coming back again and again.

One of the most exciting features of Shockwave is its capability to interactively engage the user unlike anything else on the Web. From the entertainment and advertising industry to the education and training marketplaces, the impact of Shockwave on the Internet is tremendous. Creative professionals around the world now can transform static Web pages into compelling interactive advertising, promotions, entertainment, and educational experiences for audiences of all ages. Disney's *Toy Story* Web site (http://www.toystory.com/), for example, uses Shockwave in an interactive game scenario with sounds and animations. In addition, Shockwave enables *TIME* magazine (`http://www.pathfinder.com/time/`) to create multimedia editorial pieces on the State of the Union with voice-overs and interactive graphics.

Whether used for a product demonstration, corporate training, educational lesson, online advertising, or interactive games, Shockwave opens many exciting new doors to the online world. Some examples can be seen at CNN, clnet, Advertising Age, United Airlines, Sony Music, TimeWarner, and Yahoo! To see more of these "shocked" sites, visit the Macromedia Shockwave Gallery at `http://www.macromedia.com/Tools/Shockwave/Gallery/Vanguard/` where you can experience these interactive sites and many others.

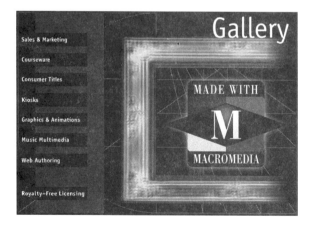

The Top Ways to Use Shockwave

Shockwave is impacting all types of content on the Web. Many leading-edge Web publishers have begun using Shockwave for a variety of applications ranging from interactive entertainment, merchandising, and advertising to education and marketing communications. As a Shockwave-savvy Web content developer, you can adapt your previously static graphics to high impact, animated, full-motion movies with built-in interactivity. Some of these main content areas include:

- High impact interfaces and consumer titles
- Online advertising and product demonstrations
- Home page animations and site bytes
- Corporate presentations
- Interactive games and virtual worlds
- Educational training and tutorials

The Insider's Perspective

What are the strengths of Shockwave?

Bruce Hunt: Three hundred thousand graphics artists and multimedia developers already know how to use Shockwave for Director. There is already a vibrant development community and the cultural infrastructure to train additional multimedia developers. Thus, Shockwave titles can be produced with the confidence that they can be maintained and enhanced.

Harry Chesley: It has a full authoring environment for multimedia development, plus a couple hundred thousand authors who can do truly amazing things with it.

Chris Walcott: Shockwave for Director has a potential user base of a quarter million people. Director provides a relatively easy way to create multimedia content.

Sarah Allen: Moving graphics, whizzy transitions, sound, and interactivity.

John Newlin: Shockwave has a very fast animation engine, the capability to mix eight channels of sound, and a fairly low overhead.

Sherri Sheridan: It animates, makes sounds, and is interactive inside Netscape 2.0.

Ken Day: It's a bridge. There's all this talent and material in Director land. There's this rich, deep technology and infrastructure on the Web. Shockwave brings the two together.

High Impact Interfaces & Consumer Titles

Before Shockwave:

High-impact interfaces used to be considered an HTML table that would adjust the text to fit a page and had blinking text. Large, uncompressed image maps were also the standard for many Web site home pages. The only consumer titles that existed were ones that you could download from an FTP site and play back using shareware.

After Shockwave:

Suddenly, the rich, visually compelling look and feel found only before as a CD-ROM interface is now available on the Web. With Shockwave, you can create an interactive environment for the user to experience and remember. For example, Pop Rocket, the makers of the "massive music video adventure game, *Total Distortion*, have successfully created an immersive online world based on this CD-ROM title. You can join the fun in their "Pop Rocket Shockwave Game Arena" (http://www.poprocket.com/shockwave/) and explore their high impact interfaces and games.

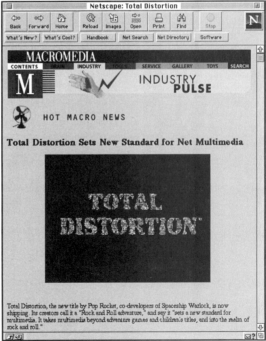

Just as the CD-ROM consumer title market took off in the mid 1980s with the advent of CD compatible PCs, you can expect to see a new method of title distribution begin as the Internet becomes the largest repository of Shockwave consumer titles. Everything from edutainment titles to science fiction games are bound to be a part of this new distribution medium.

Online Advertising & Product Demonstrations

Before Shockwave:

Advertising on the information highway used to be compromised of "billboards" of static graphics, generally in the standard small banner style (468 × 60 pixels). These banners were everywhere on Web sites, but after a while, they were rarely noticed. Product demos hardly existed (if you think about how much information you can fit in those tiny banners, you'll realize it's not that much!). Plus, there was no way to demo any product because it was just a static photograph advertisement without sound or user interaction available.

After Shockwave:

All your advertising opportunities are magnified tenfold with Shockwave. Suddenly, you can turn your standard billboards into 30-second commercials for products around the world—and in the language of your choice.

Using Shockwave you can enable your viewers to demo your product in cyberspace by allowing them to "virtually" experience it before they order. They can activate the volume buttons on a stereo, hear the fidelity of a new cellular phone, or interactively find out how to program their VCR clock without opening a manual.

Top Ways to Use Shockwave

Home Page Animations & Site Bytes

Before Shockwave:

Previously, an exciting home page consisted of large graphics, blinking text, or an old fashioned server-push/client-pull animation. And even then, the excitement often came from watching the interlaced GIF slowly draw on your screen over a 14.4 modem. Site bytes are those little icons such as "under construction" or "help" buttons that many sites include, although they seldom grab attention because static images are often overlooked.

After Shockwave:

Your home page is by far the most significant page on your Web site—it's the first page everyone goes to and remembers the most. Shockwave brings all your exciting home page ideas to life with Director's easy-to-use animation features that enable you to create captivating home pages in an instant. Animated flying logos, rotating 3D icons, and instant graphic transitions are some of the effects that can keep your home page exciting, interactive, and ever-changing. They also help to make the right first impression on your audience. And all these effects are second nature in Director!

New and improved Site Bytes add that little bit of animation or sound to your small "helper" buttons, banners, bullets, "under construction" icons, and the navigation system on your Web site. They can easily stay under 20K in most cases and are fun and easy to stack into a single Web page.

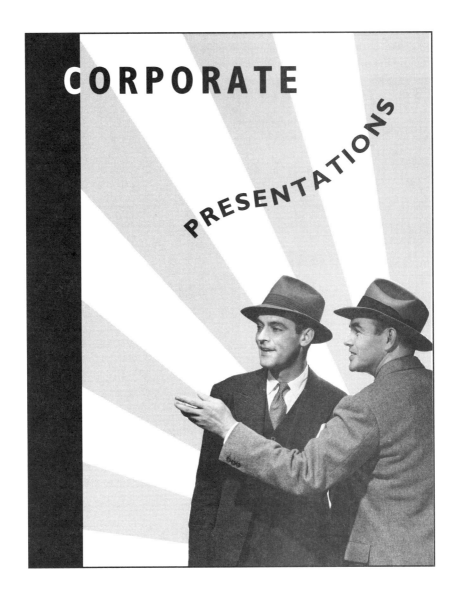

Top Ways to Use Shockwave

Corporate Presentations

Before Shockwave:

The few corporate presentations that could have existed on the Web before Shockwave were basically HTML outlines, perhaps with some interlaced graphics or charts included. Reminds one of the old overhead transparency style of presentations that we all knew so well—and sometimes fell asleep in.

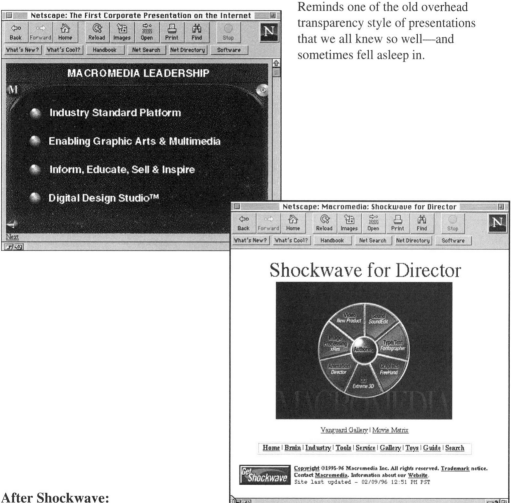

After Shockwave:

Now you can create one interactive corporate presentation, upload it to your Web site, and suddenly your entire sales force has instant access to your multimedia presentation from anywhere in the world. No longer is it necessary to carry your own expensive projection equipment and presentation hardware with you. Just log onto your Web site from anywhere in the world and give the same presentation another colleague is simultaneously presenting halfway around the world.

19

Top Ways to Use Shockwave

Interactive Games & Virtual Worlds

Before Shockwave:

Interactive games and virtual worlds for the main audience on the Internet were not possible unless one used proprietary browsers and development software. These were very costly to produce and implement on Web sites.

After Shockwave:

Now you can create fun entertainment or educational games for kids and adults to play. Complex interactive games such as Disney's *Toy Story* concentration game, Pop Rocket's *!FatShooterMan!,* and the Hands of Time's *Satan Six Pack* in addition to the standards such as simple multiplication tables, chess, blackjack, and checkers are easy to create and fun to play.

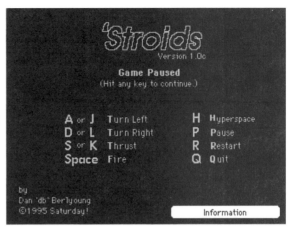

Full immersion into new virtual worlds is possible in Shockwave without the goggles. You can create your own 3D environment, including rooms and interfaces in which to explore your own cyberspace.

Top Ways to Use Shockwave

Educational Training & Tutorials

Before Shockwave:

Educational training on the Web consisted of volumes of HTML documentation perhaps with a table or graphic included. Tutorials were not seen due to the lack of interactivity on the Web before Shockwave.

After Shockwave:

You can educate your sales force and customers online with interactive training accessible from around the globe. Tutorials are now easy to keep up to date from one central facility. Shockwave training and tutorials also are great for internal corporate intra-net services to keep employees up-to-speed with minimum costs. Macromedia's specialized external and internal training courseware, like *Lingo Essentials*, for example, will eventually be delivered on the Web as online interactive tutorials around the world.

The Insider's Perspective

What's the best use for Shockwave?

Bruce Hunt: Providing an interactive experience that stimulates all the senses. Making learning about a product or subject both interesting and fun!

Harry Chesley: There is no "best use." That's like saying "what's the best use of English?" There are thousands of different uses because there are thousands of different authors and concepts and ideas.

Chris Walcott: Bringing life to an otherwise static Web page. Using small movies to take the place of .gif headers and .gif maps. Delivering sound. Interactive movies.

John Newlin: To make the world a better place. :-)

Sherri Sheridan: It's as infinite as your imagination.

Ken Day: Lord! The wonderful thing is that we don't have a clue here. The creative community will discover this for us. And it will change dramatically as bandwidths increase over the next few years.

Chapter 3
Authoring Multimedia with Shockwave

Authoring for the Internet with Director is fundamentally the same as authoring for other types of distribution. And, if you're familiar with Director, you are 90 percent of the way to being able to create Internet titles. To author a Shockwave title, you start with the Director 4.0 authoring environment on a Windows or a Macintosh machine. Then you create and test your Director movie on your local file system. After that you post-process the title through the application called Afterburner. Afterburner primarily compresses the title in order to save download time. The resulting file, renamed with the DCR extension, is placed on an HTTP Internet server for a Web browser to download to the user's machine. An HTTP server is used to serve the title across the network. Director developers need not be expert in setting up and configuring HTTP servers. As with other media types, you do need to tell the server that Director movies have a MIME type of "application/x-director" but that's all. If you are going through an Internet provider, this should be all they need to know about your media.

Authoring Ideas

In creating your movie, you can use virtually all the existing Director features, existing Director content, and all the supporting tools that you currently use to produce electronic media for import into Director. Shockwave is not a completely new authoring environment. It's a new way to package and deliver Director interactive movies.

Authoring with Shockwave offers the flexibility of Director and the distribution power of the Internet in one. Anything you create or have seen created in Director can become a Shockwave movie and subsequently be distributed over the Internet.

Art with Director Effects and Transitions

You can take existing GIF or JPEG artwork and turn it into tiny, animated movies. By importing (or even copying and pasting) your image(s) into Director, you can apply transitions, ink effects, highlights, and animation to your graphics. This is the quickest method to create Shockwave movies for a Web site. Then, after your movie is compressed, don't be surprised if your final movie is smaller than the original image you started with. Only now it's animated and interactive with Shockwave.

Re-Create Your Original Artwork

Creating new movies based on your original 24-bit artwork is another option. You can import your original artwork as a template, put it on Director's stage and re-create it by tracing it. Then delete your original artwork to save even more size by using 1-bit colored cast members.

Animated Small Buttons

You can create Director movies that have a stage size of 10 pixels by 10 pixels as simple animated bullets or hot points. They can even be interactive. You can embed three or four of these tiny movies in one page. These movies are not only tiny in size, but they load quickly and are impressive to first-time Shockwave viewers.

Make Lingo Movies

New Shockwave-specific Lingo commands have been added to allow your Director movies access to the Internet. This access can be in the form of retrieving an HTTP item or going to another Internet page. All of the new commands are described in Chapter 5.

You can use Lingo commands with your Shockwave movies to create unusual things, such as clocks with the seconds ticking in real time. Because Lingo gets the time and date from the user's machine, you won't even have to calculate time change differences. See the sample CD for more ideas and example movies.

The Basic Requirements

The following software is required to create, compress, and test your Shockwave movies (minimum requirements).

Authoring Multimedia with Shockwave

1. Macromedia Director (Windows or Macintosh)
2. The Shockwave Plug-In
3. The Afterburner post-processor compressor
4. Netscape 2.0 (Win or Mac)

The following software is recommended but not necessary:

1. Macromedia xRes or Adobe Photoshop
2. SoundEdit or SoundForge
3. Adobe Premiere

XRes or Photoshop will allow you to create professional graphics and edit images. SoundEdit and SoundForge are sound recording (sampling), editing, and looping applications. SoundEdit is recommended if you are using a Macintosh, while SoundForge is preferred if you are using a Windows machine. Premiere is used to record, edit, and play back digitally recorded video, such as QuickTime. Because QuickTime is considered linked media, Shockwave doesn't support it. However, by using Premiere you can extract the frames into PICT files. Then these frames can be imported into Director and played back in Shockwave.

What is Macromedia Director?

This book assumes that you have prior knowledge of Director—to the extent that you can open the application, create your own animated content, and save your movie. You'll find that this is the minimum knowledge necessary to understand this book. However, we highly recommend that you learn at least some basic Lingo commands before continuing. Because Lingo is supported by the Shockwave Plug-In, users will expect some level of interface control in your movies.

What is the Shockwave Plug-In?

The Shockwave Plug-In is the heart of Shockwave. The Plug-In is the Director M5 playback engine re-engineered to work within an Internet browser. Think of it as a projector engine for an Internet browser. The Plug-In needs to be installed in all your intended viewers' Internet applications. You can point them to the Macromedia home page to download it. The address is the following:

```
http://www.macromedia.com/
```

Installation instructions for Macintosh Shockwave Plug-In

1. Install Netscape Navigator 2.0.
2. Start Netscape and visit a site that contains a Shockwave movie.
3. When you get a dialog box asking to delete, save, or pick an application, choose Pick an application.
4. Select the Shockwave Plug-In.

Installation instructions for Windows Shockwave Plug-In

1. Install Netscape Navigator 2.0.
2. From the File Manager, move the shockwav.exe into an empty directory.
3. Double-click on shockwav.exe. It will unzip and leave several files including SETUP.EXE.
4. Double-click SETUP-EXE to install the Shockwave Plug-In.

Troubleshooting tips

If you install the Plug-In and are having trouble, try to find the question that best fits your situation. The following list includes some common problems with answers.

1. Does Netscape fail to serve up any Web pages at all?

   Check your network connections and Navigator installation. After you get Navigator to serve regular Web pages, go to the Shockwave Gallery and try some of the Shockwave movies there. You can reach the Gallery via the Shockwave home page at the following site:

   ```
   http://www.macromedia.com/Tools/Shockwave/index.html/
   ```

2. Do some Shockwave movies function and not others? (See answer to 3.)
3. Does a "Director error" alert box or a "Script error" alert box appear in the problem movie[s]?

   This indicates that something is wrong with the internal logic of the Director movie you're browsing. You should send email to the people who maintain the pages with the incorrectly functioning movie.

4. Do the problem movies appear as a bunch of text instead of a Shockwave movie?

   This probably means that the Web server containing the URL you're browsing has its MIME types set incorrectly. You should report this to the people who maintain the pages with the incorrectly functioning movies. They will contact their systems administrator about correcting the MIME types.

5. Does Shockwave fail to work when your machine is set to some particular display resolutions and not others?

   Be sure to contact the video card manufacturer to find out if there's an updated driver for your card. Because most cards spend several months in the distribution channel before being purchased, it's up to you to find out what the current drivers are.

6. Check to make sure that your system is set up properly.

   Windows 95:
   - Netscape Navigator version 2.0b3 or later
   - Shockwave for Director Plug-In 1.0b1 or later
   - Navigator's disk cache size set to 5 MB minimum, 10 MB preferred.

   Windows 3.1:
   - Netscape Navigator version 2.0b3 or later
   - Shockwave for Director Plug-In 1.0b1 or later
   - Navigator's disk cache size set to 5 MB minimum, 10 MB preferred
   - A bare minimum of 460K of free conventional memory before launching Windows

7. If you got this far and nothing worked, cold boot your computer and try again.
   - Exit Navigator.
   - Exit Windows and shut off the computer.
   - Wait 30 seconds and then turn the computer back on.
   - Restart Windows.
   - Launch Navigator.
   - Clear the disk cache. Go to the Options menu. Choose "Network Preferences." Click on the button that says "Clear Disk Cache Now."

8. Go to the Macromedia Shockwave Gallery and try some of the test movies there. You can reach the Gallery via the Macromedia home page at the following site:

   ```
   http://www.macromedia.com/Tools/Shockwave/index.html/
   ```

9. If the problem persists, then try to factor out exterior influences.

   The quickest way to factor out exterior influences is to temporarily strip down the operating system to its bare essentials. Under Windows 3.1, this means doing the following:
   - Comment out the LOAD= and RUN= lines of the WIN.INI file.
   - Make sure that the SHELL= line in the SYSTEM.INI file equals PROGMAN.EXE.
   - Take everything out of the Startup group.
   - Try a 640×480×256 display driver, preferably Microsoft's Super VGA 640×480×256 driver (if you know that your videocard is compatible with it), or use VGA, which is compatible with almost everything.

10. If you still haven't solved the problem, then reinstall the software.

    Be sure to quit all open applications and disable the virus protection software prior to installation.

11. Report your observations to Macromedia.

    Even if you solve the problem, please report it to them via email at: shockwavebugs@macromedia.com.

    Include as much of the following information as possible in your message, such as:
    - Your name, email address, phone, and fax numbers.
    - What's going wrong? (Any error messages.)
    - What are the precise steps to re-create the problem?
    - Your operating system and version number.
    - What is the size and type of the Windows swapfile?
    - Are there any items in the Startup group? If so, what?
    - What do the LOAD= and RUN= lines say in the WIN.INI?
    - What does the SHELL= line say in the SYSTEM.INI file?
    - Computer make and model.
    - Processor and clock rate.
    - How many megabytes of RAM does the machine have?
    - Video card make and model.
    - Display resolution and color depth.
    - Version and date of display drivers.
    - Sound card make and model.
    - Version and date of sound drivers.
    - Any other hardware connected to the system?

    They do not provide technical support through this email channel, but your problem reports help them improve the Plug-In.

The list below contains known problems with the current version of the Shockwave Plug-In. It also reflects the known problems with the Beta Windows Software. The list is included because the Plug-In is beta software and Macromedia expects some users to encounter problems. We intend for this list to help users narrow down problems.

1. Known Crashes and GPFs: Shockwave has the following crashing bugs in the current version.
    - Windows 3.1: minimum conventional memory before going into Windows must be greater than 460K, otherwise Netscape/Shockwave will crash.

2. Windows 3.1 issues:
    - Drag and drop crash—from the File Manager drag a DCR onto Navigator, drag a DIR onto Navigator, and then drag a DCR onto Navigator.
    - Restarting Win95 system while movies are playing in Navigator leads to GPF.

Authoring Multimedia with Shockwave

- Resize-maximize followed by closing Navigator leads to GPFs at some display resolutions.
- Running more than one copy of Netscape Navigator with the Shockwave Plug-In simultaneously may cause a crash.

What is the Afterburner post-processor?

Afterburner is the post-compression application that needs to be run on your finished Director movies before you load them on the Internet. Afterburner is an interface-less application that supports drag and drop. So you can simply drag the icon of your finished Director movie to the Afterburner icon, and it compresses the file or files for you. This compression process is dubbed "burning a movie" around Macromedia. The Afterburner application will ask you to rename and save the movie before it compresses it down. It will also add the DCR extension to the end of the file, which stands for Director Compressed Resource. The compression ratio is about 2:1 (40 to 60 percent). In some cases movies have compressed from 100K down to 25K. The 2:1 ratio depends on the number of sounds contained in your movie.

Afterburner does not have to be run on your Director movies every time you want to play them on the Internet. In fact, if you didn't use the Afterburner application at all, everything would still work fine. Your users would, however, be stuck with almost double the download time. Afterburner simply compresses your Director movies down as small as possible. In testing your movies, it's recommended that you skip using Afterburner. This will save you a few extra minutes of time. Make sure that you remember to compress your final, completed movie with Afterburner before you post it to the Internet. Also note that once a movie is compressed with Afterburner it can no longer be opened by Director.

The Netscape 2.0 browser

Out of the introduction of Netscape 2.0 comes Shockwave. One of the requirements of Shockwave is the Netscape 2.0 browser. There are specific technical features in Netscape 2.0 that the Shockwave Plug-In requires. And because of this, your Shockwave movies won't play in older versions of Netscape, such as version 1.1. Viewing a Shockwave movie in any version of Netscape older than 2.0 will result in a broken icon. There is, however, an HTML work-around known as the "no embed" tag. You can use this HTML tag to place a graphic (GIF or JPG) where a Shockwave movie would normally be playing in Netscape 2.0. With the Shockwave Plug-In installed, Web pages include Director movies just as existing browsers can include JPEG or GIF graphics. Director movies are included in the browser using the embed HTML tag. HTML Documents (Web pages) can include more than one Shockwave movie per page, and the movies can be scrolled while the movie continues playing.

The Insider's Perspective

Why do you think Shockwave is important?

Bruce Hunt: Shockwave is the foundation for a new Multimedia platform on the Internet. With it, the Internet will come alive with exciting, interactive, and fun experiences. The thing that is different about Shockwave is that it permits talented, non-linear thinkers (i.e. non-programmers) to provide ever-renewing multimedia experiences to an expanding audience.

Harry Chesley: It makes possible the development of commercial quality multimedia ads, articles, presentations, courseware, etc., on the Internet. This, in turn, helps to make the Net ubiquitous by pulling in more people and a wider base of people. The Net is probably the most important new communications technology of this century. Historically, more communications virtually always equals more technology and more individual freedoms.

Chris Walcott: Shockwave brings multimedia to the Web.

Sarah Allen: It's really accessible. It's a new tool that doesn't require people to learn a whole new set of skills just to put multimedia in a new place.

John Newlin: Shockwave is a good tool for showing what's possible with the Internet. I believe that we are still in the infancy of this technology. The really interesting things are still to come.

Sherri Sheridan: Shockwave is the first big step to a Snowcrash reality on the Web. Basically, it's the future of how we will live and communicate.

Keb Day: It's been said so many times that it's become trivial. It's also true. We're at a technology cusp. Communication is changing from linear forms to non-linear, interactive forms. Shockwave is a piece of that change, and one which is on the edge today. Shockwave isn't itself ground-breaking technology. This trend in communication has seeds in generations-old, printed text and late-60's computer technology. It's seen in hypertext, online doc, and an almost endless array of other examples. Shockwave is exposing existing technology in a new way (over the WWW), which enables communication that would have been prohibitively expensive to produce and distribute previously to numbers of people—who can now use it with Shockwave. Shockwave is important because it's on the edge, helping move the edge forward.

Hardware for Authoring

Shockwave development is currently limited to the Windows and/or Macintosh platforms. If you are working on one of these platforms, you basically meet the hardware requirements of Shockwave. The hardware requirements of Shockwave are 8 MB of RAM and 5 MB of free hard drive space. A color monitor is not required, but you cannot produce color movies without one. Also, if you don't have direct access to the Internet and you plan on developing for the Internet, you should consider getting a 28.8 baud modem along with an Internet access account, such as a SLIP or PPP account.

Understanding Download Times for Users

Download times are the bottleneck that you need to design your movies around. Use this simple equation: "Movie size equals download time." Therefore, the larger you make your Director movies, the longer it will take to load and play them over the Internet. Most users sign onto the Internet with a 14,400 baud modem or less. For this simple reason, you should develop your movies to be as small as possible (even before applying the Afterburner compressor).

The chart below shows theoretical download times for different speed modems and connection types. The table takes into consideration server performance, serial-link overhead, and modem-to-channel capacity overhead. The author's connection to the Internet is via a T3 line (not represented in the chart). The T3 line is the single largest connection available. It has the bandwidth equivalent of 1,500 28.8 baud modems or 45 MegBits per second of throughput.

Download Table

	Modems		ISDN T1 line	
Size	*14.4Kbs*	*28.8Kbs*	*64Kbs*	*1.5Mbit*
30K	30 sec	10 sec	6 sec	1 sec
100K	180 sec	90 sec	20 sec	1 sec
200K	300 sec	180 sec	40 sec	1 sec
500K	15 min.	7.5 min.	90 sec	3 sec
1M	30 min.	15 min.	180 sec	6 sec

If you plan to develop a movie over 300K (after Afterburner compression is applied), you might consider loading a smaller movie first and then using the GoToNetMovie lingo command to load the larger file. New Lingo commands will be discussed later.

Determining File Size

The file size of your movie should be constantly monitored as you continue working. This way your final movie size will not come as a shock to you, and it's easier to fix as you go along.

If you are trying to determine the exact size of your movie, you can use the Get Info window (Command-I) in the Macintosh finder (see Figure 3.1). When you open this window you'll notice two sizes under the size heading. This happens because the file really has two different sizes. The first size description is the space the file is taking up on your hard disk. The second size description, in parentheses, is the important one. This description is the actual file size used in bytes. It is this amount of data that is transmitted via modem.

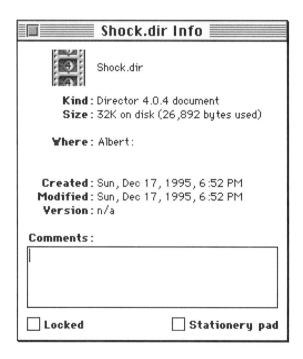

Figure 3.1   *The Get Info window is where you'll find the exact size of your files.*

The Insider's Perspective

What impact do you foresee for Shockwave in the future Internet community?

Bruce Hunt: It enhances the humanization of the Internet by providing the means to create visual, aesthetic, interactive experiences. Things no longer have to be dry, lifeless text, but can now be an integrated expression of visual content, motion, sound, and words to create a stimulating interactive environment where the audience can participate and control the presentation of information. It has the potential to be both garish and ugly, as well as elegant and sublime. It has the potential to infuriate and enthrall—in short, to excite and ultimately teach while being entertaining. It may enhance the building of multimedia communities by providing many more options for their construction and opening the construction to another level of creativity.

Harry Chesley: It will help bring the mass consumer onto the Net. The mass culture will eventually overrun the existing Internet culture as the dominant culture on the Net—which is unfortunate but inevitable.

Chris Walcott: Massive impact.

Sarah Allen: I expect that Shockwave will grow with its users. We learn from what people do with it and can add features and update the product accordingly. I think the Internet provides the possibility for new kinds of software development cycles where user-feedback is much more readily available and will contribute to much cooler software.

John Newlin: I think that in the short term, Shockwave is going to be something people see as "pretty cool," but it won't be used extensively. In the long term I think it, or something like it, will be adopted as the de facto multimedia tool for the Internet. Of course, with the Internet.

Sherri Sheridan: It's going to turn people's computers into interactive TVs.

Chapter 4

New Director Authoring Techniques for Shockwave

The new authoring techniques described in this chapter are designed to give your movies the maximum impact with the least amount of file size overhead. To accomplish this, you must decide before you create your movies if they are going to be Shockwave movies. The standard method of Director development for a CD-ROM or other target platform is inefficient for Shockwave. That is not to say, ineffective for their specific design. Shockwave authoring is simply a higher discipline of Director development.

The authoring techniques described in this chapter consist of the following: image dithering, audio downsampling, Cast window and Score window tips, and saving and compressing your finished movie. You'll also find a discussion of content creation tips. Since content can be created anywhere, you can use applications like Macromedia xRes or Adobe Photoshop to create images, Extreme 3D or Infini-D to create animation, and SoundEdit or SoundForge to create audio. Then you can import all your content into Director for use as a Shockwave movie.

Image Tips

Images are defined as anything that is imported into Director and can be opened in Director's Paint window (Command-5). This includes PICs animation sequences and any text that you convert to bitmap.

Remember, you are no longer developing content that is used in the normal Director fashion. If you are creating in Photoshop, try to do as much as possible to save image size while you are working. Crop your image[s] as tightly as possible and try color reduction techniques and effects, such as posterize. Then save your final images as index color.

When you choose index color from the mode menu, a dialog box will come up and offer you many color options. You should choose the following: 8-bit, system palette, and diffusion dither. Choosing index color will convert your image down to 256 colors from the system's normal palette. Any colors the system palette is missing should be dithered as closely as possible to the original, even though the index color window offers you smaller color reduction bit depths, such as 4-bit, 2-bit, or even 1-bit. Don't use any of them except for 1- or 8-bit. For example, 4- and 2-bit color palettes do not contain enough of the standard colors used by the Macintosh or PC. Consequently, they could cause unexpected and unusual palette shifts when your movie is being played back. This could, however, be looked at as an effect. You will need to be the final judge.

If you are creating 3D animation for Shockwave, be very careful of size. Most 3D applications are designed to give you smooth playback and rich photo-realistic images. Smooth playback is accomplished by rendering a great number of frames or images. Photo-realistic images contain 32-bits of information—24-bits of color information plus an 8-bit alpha channel. One single 32-bit image at 640×480 pixels can contain 16.7 million different colors and can take up to 1.2 MB of disk space. This amount alone would take about 20 minutes to download via modem. This fact may indicate that 3D animation is out of the question—and to some degree it is. However, there are still many ways you can use 3D animation. Most animation applications enable you to control the output color depth and the output shading depth. You can try using less than photo-realistic quality. For example, 3D wireframe renderings only contain two colors and can be dithered to 1-bit. This will drastically save on file size. You can also lower the number of total frames rendered. For example, if you are rendering 2 seconds of animation, don't render at 30FPS (frames per second). Instead, you can lower the number to 15 or even 12FPS. This lower number will result in slightly choppier animation but will give you drastic file size savings.

Anything you can do to reduce the size of your content before you import it into Director will help with the download bottleneck most users face.

Thinking Small

The first step in creating a Shockwave movie is to think small. This fact cannot be stressed enough. The main advantage of small movie creation is that you'll have reduced download time and increased playback performance. When you think about content, also think about how you can keep the content small.

The following steps are recommended when creating content for Shockwave:

- ◆ Dither all your cast members to 8-bit or less.
- ◆ Don't use audio samples above 8-bit, 22.5 Khz.
- ◆ Use colored, 1-bit cast members as often as possible.
- ◆ Crop redundant or unused colors in cast members.
- ◆ Use ink effects and transitions to alter, not duplicate, cast members.
- ◆ Delete all cast members before saving.

Cast Member Dithering

Dithering an image is an automatic operation that is designed to reduce the number of colors contained within an image. This task is normally done to save file size. Take a look at Figure 4.1. This image shows a normal 24-bit, undithered image. Figure 4.2 shows the same image dithered to the Macintosh 8-bit system palette. As you can see, there is a difference in the images. The undithered image looks better; however, the dithered image is about 50% smaller in file size. Saving on your file size is more important than quality for Shockwave movies. Internet users simply won't download movies that take too long to load.

Figure 4.1   *An undithered 24-bit image.*

Figure 4.2   *A dithered 8-bit image.*

Macromedia Shockwave for Director

Cast member dithering is necessary when your imported images were originally designed in 16-, 24-, or 32-bit color. Dithering in Director can be done during import or after. The recommended method for Shockwave is during import. This will prevent a cast member from being left at an unnecessarily high color depth. Import dithering only takes place at or below 8-bit color. Follow these steps to activate import dithering:

1. Open the monitors control panel.
2. Set the color depth to 256 colors or less.
3. Start Director and import your images.

Regardless of the prior color depth of your images, they are automatically dithered to 8 bits or lower during import, depending on your monitor's color depth setting.

Dithering can also take place inside the Paint or Cast window. When you use the Paint window, you can only dither one cast member at a time. This is unlike the Cast window, where you can dither multiple cast members at a time. Here's how to do it:

1. Open the Paint window (Command-5).
2. Double-click the color depth indicator (see Figure 4.3).
3. Choose 8-bit from the color depth pop-up menu.
4. Click OK.

Figure 4.3 *Double-click here to set the color depth.*

In the Cast window you have the same dithering controls as the Paint window, except you can affect more than one cast member at a time. This is great if you accidentally import images at the wrong color depth.

New Director Authoring Techniques for Shockwave

To dither multiple cast members at one time, use the transform bitmap option from the cast menu. Here are the steps:

1. Open the Cast window (Command-3).
2. Select all the cast members that you wish to change.
3. Choose "transform bitmap" from the cast menu.
4. Choose 8-bit from the color depth pop-up menu.

Tip

You can Shift-click on as many cast members as you like, or you can Command-click on cast members out of order.

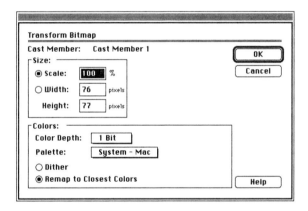

Figure 4.4   *This window sets cast member color depth.*

If you are planning to dither cast members to 1-bit instead of 8-bit, there are a few additional techniques you will want to be aware of.

Special 1-Bit Techniques

Dithering cast members to 1-bit offers the greatest file size savings and still allows for color. Most users are unaware of the fact that Director can dither cast member(s) to 1-bit and still allow for color. The steps to dither your cast member to 1-bit are the same for any other color depth. In Director you can dither in the Cast window or the Paint window. For example, if you are working in the Paint window and you want to dither to 1-bit color follow these steps:

1. Double-click the color depth indicator (refer to Figure 4.3).
2. Select 1-bit from the pop-up menu.
3. Choose Dither or Remap to Closest Colors.
4. Click OK.

The Dither and Remap buttons have a very different effect on 1-bit image conversion. We recommend using the remap option. When you choose the dither option, Director assumes that you want the image to look as true to the original as possible, which causes color substitution and replacement. For example, 1-bit cast members can only have color assigned to them when the color black is used. After you remap your cast member(s) to 1-bit black, simply drag it/them to the stage.

You assign the color to the cast member on the stage by using the Tools window foreground color chip (see Figure 4.5).

1. Drag your cast member onto the stage or into the Score.
2. Open the Score window (Command-4) and select the cast member.
3. Open the Tools window (Command-7) and choose the foreground color of your choice.

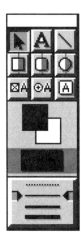

Figure 4.5 *Use the Tools window to change the foreground color of a sprite.*

You can select a new color for every different frame the cast member is in. Changing color in each frame causes your users to believe you have numerous, different colored cast members in your movie.

Don't forget that 1-bit color remapping also works on text. Whether you copy and paste your text from an external application or create it in Director, you can remap it to any color. When you create text, it becomes a text cast member. To convert it, open the Cast window and choose Convert to Bitmap from the cast menu. This action converts all your text to a 1-bit cast member. From here, place your text on the stage and use the foreground color chip to alter the color.

New Director Authoring Techniques for Shockwave

Cropping Unused Color and Text

If you are using large images as backgrounds or as banner graphics, you should consider cropping the most redundant color used in the graphic. Changing your entire stage to the cropped color will fill in the holes. Or you can leave the stage alone and create a single 1-bit cast member, assigning it the color of your cropped color. There are two methods you can use to accomplish this. Take a look at Figure 4.6. It shows a normal image with a large surrounding color. By using the eraser tool in the Paint window, you can delete the unused portion of the color, making the image look more like Figure 4.7.

Figure 4.6   *A normal 13.5K image.*

Figure 4.7   *A color, cropped 8K image.*

The other technique you can use is the Switch Colors option in the Paint window. By visually looking at your image and determining the most redundant color, you can delete it using the Switch Colors option. Open your cast member in the Paint window and follow these steps to switch colors:

1. Find and select the most redundant color with the eyedropper tool.
2. Select the image by double-clicking on the top, right-hand selection tool.
3. Choose Switch Colors from the effects menu.

After following these steps, the color you selected with the eyedropper tool is switched to white. Because the color white is the background color for the background transparent ink effect, you can have any color show through the white area when it's placed on the stage.

The same techniques can be applied to text cast members. If you create or import any text for use in a Shockwave movie, pick a font that is common, such as Times or Helvetica. Picking a common font is necessary if you do not use the Convert to Bitmap option. Text you create with the text tool (Command-7) takes up much less space than text that you convert to bitmap. For this reason, always try to use the text tool to create your text. If you need to use a font that is not very common you must convert it to a bitmap graphic. Make sure that you also dither it to 1-bit to save space.

Audio Techniques

Audio can add dramatic impact to your Director movie. However, if you are not careful, it can also add a gigantic amount of size to your movie as well. By understanding a few basic techniques, you can save a lot of unnecessary file size. Here are some techniques you can use.

First, you should downsample all your audio to 8-bit, 22.5 Khz or less. Your movies will be exceeding the quality limits of most personal computers' internal speakers if you use audio above 8-bit, 22.5 Khz.

Second, create small audio samples and loop them instead of using larger sounds. When you want a background beat or music of some sort in your movie, edit the sample so that it loops. This way, for example, you can play a small 20K sound throughout your movie instead of playing a 200K sound.

You can have as many sounds as you like inside a Shockwave movie. A Shockwave movie can even be sound only, if you like. Creating a sound-only Shockwave movie will cause a sound to play and/or loop when someone first enters your page on the Internet. Because HTML documents can include more than one Shockwave movie per page, you need to be aware of when and where you use sound in your movies. For example, if you have two Shockwave movies embedded into one HTML page and they both have audio tracks, the Internet browser is going to get confused about which audio track to play. You need to design the movies so that only one audio track is playing at a time or allow the user to click on the movie to start and stop the audio from playing.

Audio Downsampling Techniques

You should always use 11 or 22 Khz sample rates. Any nonstandard sample rates, such as 7 or 5 Khz, will actually alter the pitch of the playing sound on some computers.

Audio samples are going to be the largest contributing factor to movie file size. By using this formula, you can determine your quality versus time factor:

(sample rate) times (the length of the sample) equals (Audio file size)

This formula is for a mono sound file. A stereo sample is a redundant waste of space and not recommended for Shockwave. This formula can be used to help you determine how long (in time) your audio samples can be, before you record them. If, for example, you have allocated 50K of space in your Shockwave movie for audio, you can use the formula backward to determine the length your sample can be [50 / (your sample rate) = (max time)].

For example:

Backward usage of the formula:

(50K of space) at (11.127 Khz) equals (4.5 Seconds).

(50) / (11.127) = (4.5)

Forward usage of the formula:

A (22.5 Khz sample) at (5 seconds) requires (112.5K) of disk space.

(22.5) * (5) = (112.5)

A 5 second sample at 11.5 Khz only requires 57.5K of disk space. This could save 30 seconds during the download process depending on the user's connection speed.

Make sure that you use a sound editing application that gives you the capability to edit the audio waveform, normalize audio, edit the sample rate of the file, and set loop in and out points. You'll also need to save your audio in the AIFF sound format for the Mac and the WAV format for the PC. We recommend SoundEdit Pro for the Macintosh. SoundEdit Pro not only does all of the above, but it also copies and pastes sounds between Director's Cast window. Copying and pasting your sounds, instead of saving and importing, will help save you valuable time.

Before you downsample your audio you will want to crop unused space from it. Figure 4.8 shows a normal audio sample.

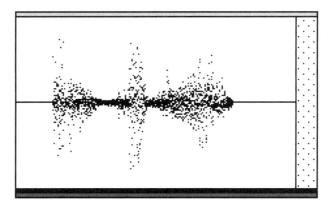

Figure 4.8   *Audio waveform with lead-in and lead-out time.*

However, for Shockwave purposes, Figure 4.8 is actually a bad example. Figure 4.8 shows a 2-second audio sample that has almost half a second of silence at the start and end of the file. This lead-in and lead-out lag time should be deleted until it looks more like Figure 4.9.

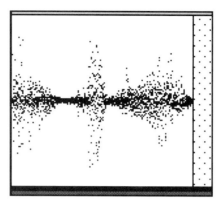

Figure 4.9 *Audio waveform with lead-in and lead-out time removed.*

This technique is known as cropping or editing the audio waveform. After the sample is cropped as tightly as possible, it needs to be normalized. Make sure that you normalize only the finished, cropped sample. The process of normalization makes the sample as loud as possible without introducing distortion. The volume level is based on the entire sample's volume. Therefore, applying the normalization effect before you crop your sample could result in less than 100% utilization of the effect.

The next step in editing is adjusting the sample rate of the file. Adjusting the sample rate can save you 10's or 100's of K in disk space, but at the expense of quality. Your target or ideal sample rate is 11.025 at 8 bits. You shouldn't go any smaller than this. Any sample rates below 11.025 can confuse less expensive sound boards on PC's. The boards tend to interpret, for example, a 7 Khz sample back up to 11 Khz, thus transposing the playback pitch up one or two octaves and making the sample playback too fast. Because Shockwave movies are targeted for the Internet, you, as a developer, do not know what the final playback machine will be, and therefore must develop for the weakest machine in the Internet chain. Most of the time you can simply choose to set the sample rate at 11.025 Khz, let the application downsample the sound, and then just save the file. There may be times when the sample sounds untrue to the original sample or just not good enough after downsampling. In this case you have two options.

Option One:

1. Leave the sample at the higher 22.050 Khz setting and try to make up the difference somewhere else in the movie.
2. Use effects to alter the downsampled audio (provided the sound application you selected has them). Some effects, such as an equalizer or emphasizer might help boost the high notes that are stripped out during the downsampling.

New Director Authoring Techniques for Shockwave

Tip

If you are using SoundEdit Pro you can alter the octave of the sample before you downsample, which helps improve the high notes and tones.

Option Two:
1. Select the entire sample (Command-A).
2. Choose Shift Pitch from the Effects menu.
3. Set the pitch down one full octave (12 notes on the keyboard). Click OK.
4. Downsample the audio to 11Khz.
5. Select the entire sample (Command-A).
6. Choose Shift Pitch from the Effects menu.
7. Set the pitch up one full octave. Click OK.

This should preserve some of the higher notes and tones normally lost to dithering.

Audio Looping Techniques

It's a good idea to use audio loops as often as possible. However, Shockwave movies programmed to loop indefinitely can tie up the processor and cause problems for the user. Therefore, we recommend that you program the movie to stop playing the audio after a given number of loops or give the user control to stop and start the audio.

Finding and creating the loop in and loop out points takes some practice. If you are able to drag the loop points back and forth on your sample, you will have a much easier time finding the loop. There is no real trick to finding a point because every audio sample is different. After you get the sample looping the way you like it, crop the rest of the sample and save only the looping portion of the file.

Now that you've saved your sample, import it into Director (Command-J). Notice that the sound comes in as an audio cast member. Check its size by double-clicking on it in the Cast window. When the cast member dialog comes up, you can check its size, play the sample, and enable or disable the loop option. With the loop option unchecked, the sample will play one time and then stop. With it checked, the sample will play until you quit the movie or use Lingo commands to stop it. Don't use any of the Wait for commands in the tempo channel to start and stop your movie or sounds. They are disabled in Shockwave. If you need to "wait for" a sound to finish playing before proceeding to the next frame, use the Lingo Soundbusy command. Open the Score window, click in the script channel, and start typing. The action of typing will open the Score window's script window. Enter the following Lingo command:

```
on exitframe
  if SoundBusy(X) then go (the frame)
end
```

The X should be replaced by the channel number that your sound is in, inside the Score window—either a 1 or a 2.

Another method of looping a sound using Lingo gives the stopping control to the user. Enter the following Lingo commands in the script window:

```
on exitframe
  go (the frame)
end

on mousedown
  go to the frame +1
end
```

Your Director movie will stop on this frame (playing your looping sound) until the mouse is clicked on the movie. The mouseDown Lingo command is set to take your movie to the next frame. You can replace this command with a go marker() command if you want to go to a specific marker that you created.

Turning Sound On/Off in Movies

Often during movie creation you'll want the capability to turn off your audio. It can become annoying to listen to your sample over and over hundreds of times while you are working. To turn off a specific channel, simply open the Score window and click the radio button next to the channel number (see Figure 4.10).

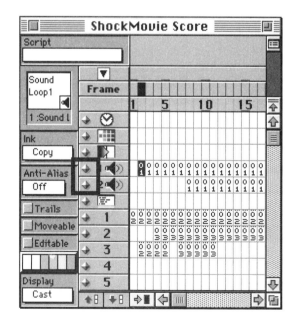

Figure 4.10   *Click the on/off button(s) in the Score to test your audio.*

New Director Authoring Techniques for Shockwave

To turn the channel back on, click the same radio button again. You can click as many of these radio buttons as you like. Just remember to turn them all back on before you save your final movie.

The radio button method of turning sound off is good for testing audio samples that are in different channels. If you can't hear the sound in channel 2 very well, turn off channel 1. If you're simply trying to shut off all sound, use the Control panel window's global sound button (see Figure 4.11).

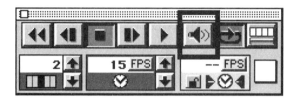

Figure 4.11 *Click the global on/off button to test your movie with no audio.*

We recommend that you give "global audio control" to your users. This can only be done through the use of a Lingo statement. One of the best methods is to open the movie script window (Command-Shift-U) and type the following:

```
on mousedown
   set the soundenabled to not (the soundenabled)
end
```

This statement tells the sound-enabled property to switch to the opposite setting.

The mouseDown handler in the above script is activated whenever the mouse button is down or clicked once. The Lingo property "the SoundEnabled" determines whether the sound in your movie is on or off. Use this in all your movies that contain audio. Make sure to inform your users that they can click to disable the audio as well.

Cast and Score Tips

Working on a Shockwave movie requires very precise control over the size of every single cast member. Because of this, it's a good idea to have some order to your Cast window. Grouping your cast members together by size is the best method. Size grouping your images, text, and audio cast members together will help you keep precise track of cast member sizes. First, group all the cast members that take 0 to 10K of space, and then group all the cast members that take 11 to 50K of space. This will allow you to see where the bulk of your movie size is going.

The Cast window also has an option for selecting the thumbnail size of the Cast window's images. We recommend that you set it to the lowest setting "small" in order to help you see more of your cast members.

After you start placing cast members on the stage, you should also start experimenting with different ink effects and transitions. You can use different ink effects on two Score window copies of the same cast member. This will give you the appearance of two different cast members without adding more size to your movie. You can use transitions to simulate the motion of cast members. Using transitions can be faster and smoother than in-betweening the motion yourself. Using a transition to move your cast member also gives you control over the speed of the motion path. This is more powerful than the traditional in-betweening method used in the Score window.

The Score window only has a few options that you need for Shockwave movie development. One of the options, colored cells, should be used during authoring. Coloring cells allows you to colorize your cast members by size. Make the color red represent the larger size cast members and so on. By using colors, you'll visually be able to see where the bulk of your cast member size is coming from, and it will help you determine if any preloading might be necessary.

Ink and Transition Techniques

You should only experiment with different ink effects when you are not working on a specific Shockwave movie. By experimenting this way, you'll know exactly what ink effects do before you start working.

Open Director and create a dozen or so cast members in the Paint window. Make sure that you use different colors and different shapes. Then drag all your cast members on the stage. Some of your cast members should overlap one another. Now you can either open the Score window and apply different inks to each cast member, or you can simply Command-click on each cast member to open the ink pop-up menu for that cast member.

Try experimenting with Not Ghost, Reverse, Subtract, and other ink effects. Try using a black background with the different inks. Because there are so many different ink effects and each one can look different depending on the color of the cast member, try as many as you have time for. Before you delete a cast member because it doesn't look good, try applying a new ink effect. Don't underestimate the power of a good ink effect!

Here are some things you can do with inks.

- ◆ Make the background color of any cast member transparent, regardless of what color it is.
- ◆ You can make two overlapping colors reverse.
- ◆ Create an image or cast member that can only be seen over a black background or black cast member.

For a great visual description of what each ink effect actually looks like, check out the back of your tips and tricks manual that came with your Director packaging.

After you choose the ink effects you like, try using transitions to animate them. Developers often overlook using transition as a means of animating their cast members. By using transitions that actually move the cast member, you can animate your cast members in one frame.

1. Drag your cast member to the stage.
2. Choose the transition channel in the Score. Open the transition window by double-clicking in the transition channel.
3. Type the first letter of the name of the transition. Press "P" for the push series of transitions. The Push down transition should have been automatically selected for you. This transition will allow you to animate the arrival of your cast member. It has controls for duration and chunk size, which allow you to control the speed at which your cast member is pushed on the screen. Play with the duration, not the chunk size, if you want to adjust the speed. The chunk size can simply be left at its default setting.

Movie Control Techniques

Give your movies starting and stopping controls if they loop continuously. Users will appreciate this level of control, and it will make your movies interactive. A simple global Lingo command can be used in the movie script of all your Shockwave movies. Open the movie script window (Command-Shift-U) and type the following:

```
on mousedown
  if (the pausestate) = 0 then pause
  else
    continue
  end if
end
```

This Lingo handler will check to see if the movie is currently paused and then pause the movie if it wasn't stopped already. The next time that you click, the movie will continue playing. Remember that this handler, if placed in the movie script, will affect your entire movie—no matter where you are. So, if you are planning to make your movie more interactive than this, you might want to rename the "mouseDown" handler to "myhandlername." Then you can put a button on the stage of your movie and call "myhandlername" to pause and unpause your movie.

The other option is not to give control to your users. Instead, you can make your movie pause for a few seconds on a key frame that you pick, perhaps one that shows your company's logo. The following Lingo handler will pause your movie in one frame.

```
on exitframe
set time to X
   if (the timer) > (time * 70) then starttimer
   if (the timer) < (time * 60) then go to the frame
end
```

You can change the (X) to your desired pause length and then put this handler in one frame in the Score. Your movie will run until it hits this script, and then it will continue after the number of seconds expires.

Cast Conservation Techniques

At this point your movie should be tiny, user-friendly, and ready for compressing. One last step is necessary to ensure that your movie is as small as possible—the removal of all unused cast members. Deleting all your unused cast members is a simple operation. To delete, simply open your Cast window and then choose Find Cast Members from the cast menu or type Command-;. This command will open the Find Cast Members dialog box (see Figure 4.12). Click the "that are not used in the score" radio button. Then click the Select button. Your Cast window will automatically open and have all the cast members that are not used in your score selected. You can simply choose Clear Cast Members from the Edit menu to delete them.

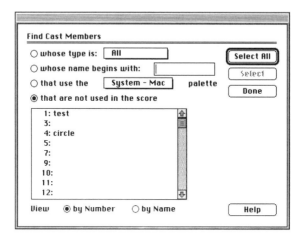

Figure 4.12 *Use the Find Cast window to find unused cast members.*

Before you delete your cast members that are not used in the Score, make sure that you look at every one of them. Because Lingo commands and handlers are stored as cast members, they will be deleted because they are not used in the Score. Make sure that you Command-click these off so that they are not selected.

Saving and Compressing Techniques

At this point you are ready to save your final movie. Normally, in Director you just "save" and you're done. For Shockwave movies the authors have learned a little different technique that seems to save even more space. Not always, though. Here is the process:

- Make sure that you have all your cast members dithered to 8-bit or less. You should also delete any unused cast members and save your movie disk.
- Now, choose Save and Compact. You'll save your file to disk in the order that it appears in the Score window. Then choose Save as and rename your movie to something else. It is this file that you'll use as your finished movie.
- At this point, you're ready to add Lingo commands and/or compress your finished Director movie into a Shockwave movie.

Macromedia Developer Profile

Name: Harry Chesley
Title: Senior Architect

How did you get involved on the Shockwave team?

I was hired in January, 1995 to make Director work with networks. I started the Shockwave project shortly after that.

What is your greatest contribution to Shockwave?

The name and the overall architecture.

What is the coolest thing about Shockwave?

The Director authors.

What is the "uncoolest" thing about Shockwave?

That this was probably how it felt to develop commercial TV.

What is the one thing you would change in Shockwave if you had enough time?

I'd get rid of the Macromedia logo that it displays while downloading a movie.

What is your favorite Shockwave Easter egg?

The blue and purple one.

What one word (other than "shocking") describes your experience with Shockwave?

Exhausting.

What one statement typifies your experiences during the Shockwave product cycle?

"I don't do drugs. I just don't sleep." — Janis Joplin

How long have you been at Macromedia?

One year.

Where were you working before?

Apple, for eight years.

What did you do?

Hypermedia, communications, HyperCard Toolkits, Rumor Monger, PowerTalk... .

One interesting fact about you?

I've never been to Japan.

What about your screensaver?

Actually, there's a story there: It started with an app named NavCom.

But even before that, it started when the movie 2001 came out while I was in high school. I loved the movie. But mostly I loved the background displays in the spaceships. I always wanted displays like that for myself. One day I realized I could have them on my Mac.

I wrote a little app called NavCom that put up 32×32 pixel windows that you could scatter around your screen. The windows alternate random displays: three letter abbreviations, graphs, star constellations, core dumps, etc. And they change all the time, in the background on the Mac. I find that some people (like me) love them—they give you a feeling of stuff happening all the time on your machine. But other people hate the constant movement in the corner of their eye. Then After Dark came out. They did a good job of setting it up so you could write a screen saver module yourself: you just call QuickDraw to draw in the rectangle they give you. Using QuickDraw is pretty easy, so you're really just limited by your imagination. I took the graphing algorithm I'd used in NavCom and wrote an After Dark module called GraphStat. In addition to grids and lines, it also puts up random labels by randomly picking one word from each of three word lists and sticking them together. It won a prize (a tape backup unit) in an After Dark contest. I also have another After Dark module called Orbitron that shows planetary orbits. It actually shows where the planets are right now and where they're going.

Your greatest accomplishment?

Hasn't happened yet, I hope.

What are the longest number of continuous hours you have worked at Macromedia?

Who keeps track?

What's the worst Shockwave tagline you have heard?

Who keeps track?

What is the longest wait you've had for a download? Was it worth it?

Who keeps track?

How many hours do you surf per day?

Who keeps track? :-)

Do you drink tea or coffee? And how many cups per day?

Mountain Dew, the one true drink of programmers.

Chapter 5

Lingo Commands for Shockwave

With the introduction of Shockwave come new Lingo commands specifically designed for Shockwave movies only. In fact, they are so new, when you use them in Director, you will get script errors if you try to activate them. This simple fact is going to make testing your movies difficult. You cannot be sure that your Lingo works until after your movies are actually running in a browser, such as Netscape. This may be time-consuming. Until Macromedia releases a workaround, there is nothing else that can be done.

New Shockwave Lingo Commands

It may be difficult to test the accuracy of your Lingo commands; however, the benefit of using these new commands is well worth the trouble. You can have a Director movie display your company logo and a button that says, for example, "Click Here." Attach the Lingo command GoToNetPage as a script to the "Click Here" button, and your users will have the ability to open any HTTP location on the Net. This is all done within the Director movie. You also can use the PreLoadNetThing script to load another HTTP location into the local disk cache of the user's machine. When they are ready to open the HTTP location it is read instantly from disk. This is an excellent way to preload larger Director movies in the background, too.

The following chapter describes the new Lingo commands available to Shockwave movies. These commands give your movies the ability to access the Internet network.

The Internet is described as an asynchronous place. That means that it takes time to send and receive information from the Net. However, during a download, users can continue interacting with your Shockwave movie. The new Shockwave Lingo commands involve starting an asynchronous operation with one command, checking to see if the operation has been completed with another, and finally getting the results of the operation from yet another command. In other words, three separate commands deliver one operation. This is different from normal Lingo commands, which are designed to immediately return the result. Lingo commands that appear in the "Courier font" are exact commands or handlers that can be copied word for word.

GoToNetPage (URI)

This command opens a URI (Uniform Resource Identifier). It can be a Director movie or any other MIME type, such as a graphic. Using this command will open a new HTTP page within your Internet browser.

Syntax:

```
GoToNetPage (" string ")
```

Example 1:

This example opens a Net page when the mouse is clicked.

```
on mousedown
  GoToNetPage (" http://www.yourserver.com ")
end
```

Example 2:

This example, if put in the Score, will automatically open a URI for you, when your movie reaches this frame.

```
on exitframe
  GoToNetPage (" http://www.yourserver.com ")
end
```

GoToNetMovie (URI)

This command retrieves and starts a new Director movie. The new movie occupies the same display area as the current calling movie.

Syntax:

```
GoToNetMovie (" string ")
GoToNetMovie (" string#marker ")
```

Example 1:

This example opens a Shockwave movie named "movie1.dcr" when the mouse is clicked.

```
on mousedown
  GoToNetMovie (" http://www.yourserver.com/movie1.dcr ")
end
```

Example 2:

This example demonstrates another feature of this command—the ability to open a different movie and choose to go to a marker within that movie. Assume that the movie titled "movie1.dcr" contains a marker named "SW."

```
on mousedown
  GoToNetMovie(" http://www.server.com/movie1.dcr#SW ")
end
```

GetNetText (URI)

This asynchronous command starts the retrieval of an HTTP item. The item is read by Lingo as text. Currently, only HTTP URLs are supported as valid URI parameters. This command only starts the retrieval; see the NetTextResults command for putting the result of the retrieval.

Syntax:

```
GetNetText (" string ")
```

Example 1:

This example starts the retrieval of the text from the specified HTTP location when the mouse is clicked.

```
on mousedown
  GetNetText (" http://www.yourserver.com ")
end
```

Example 2:

This example checks the current time, and if it is 3:00 PM, loads text from an Internet HTTP location into the local disk cache. Remember that you can blend old and new Lingo together anytime.

```
on idle
  if (the time) = "3:00 PM" then
    GetNetText (" http://www.yourserver.com ")
  end if
end
```

PreLoadNetThing (URI)

This asynchronous command starts the preloading of an HTTP item into the local cache file. The HTTP item loaded can be anything—including a Director movie, an HTML page, or a graphic. Currently, only HTTP URLs are supported as part of the URI parameters. In general, any item that has been preloaded can be viewed instantly because it's being loaded from the local cache file. However, it's impossible to determine when the item gets removed from the local cache file.

Syntax:

```
PreLoadNetThing (" string ")
```

Example 1:

This example preloads an HTTP page into the local cache file when the mouse is clicked.

```
on mousedown
  PreLoadNetThing (" http://www.yourserver.com ")
end
```

Example 2:

This example script is designed to be attached to a frame in the Score. This script will automatically load a Net page for you.

```
on enterframe
  PreLoadNetThing(" http://www.yourserver.com ")
end
```

NetDone ()

This command is used to check the state of an asynchronous operation, such as PreLoadNetThing. Specifically, this function returns "true" or 1 when the asynchronous network operation is completed. Until that point the command returns "false" or 0.

Syntax:

```
NetDone ( text )
```

Example 1:

This example checks to see if an asynchronous operation has finished every time the mouse is clicked. The resulting answer is put into a text field named "status."

```
on mousedown
  if NetDone = 1 then put "OK" into field "status"
  if NetDone <> 1 then put "Still Loading" into field "status"
end
```

Example 2:

This example checks the status of the NetDone result and beeps the machine twice when it's OK.

```
on mousedown
  if NetDone = 1 then beep 2
end
```

NetError ()

This function is used to test whether an asynchronous network operation is finished. The function returns an empty string until the network operation is finished. Then it returns an "OK" if the operation was completed, or it will return a string describing the error.

Syntax:

```
NetError ( text )
```

Example:

In this example, when the mouse is clicked the NetError function is tested, and the result is put in a text field named "status."

```
on mousedown
  put NetError into field "status"
end
```

NetTextResult ()

This function returns the text-only result from the "GetNetText" operation. The result will be the text from an HTTP page. The NetTextResult function can only be called when the NetDone or NetError commands report that the operation is complete. Shockwave discards the results of the previous operation in order to conserve memory.

Syntax:

```
NetTextResult ( text )
```

Example 1:

This example puts the result of the "GetNetText" command into a text filed named "status."

```
on mousedown
  put NetTextResult into field "status"
end
```

Example 2:

This example uses both commands in one mouseDown handler. This might not be a good idea unless the HTTP item you are accessing is very quick.

```
on mousedown
  GetNetText (" http://www.yourserver.com ")
  put NetTextResult into field "status"
end
```

Macromedia Shockwave for Director

NetMime ()

This function is a simple test operation that returns the MIME type of the HTTP item previously called by an asynchronous command. The NetMime function can only be called when the NetDone or NetError commands report that the operation is complete. Shockwave discards the results of the previous operation in order to conserve memory.

Syntax:

```
NetMime ( text )
```

Example 1:

This example puts the MIME type in a field named "status."

```
on mousedown
  put NetMime into field "status"
end
```

Example 2:

This example puts both the MIME type and the text from the HTTP item into a field named "status."

```
on mousedown
  put "The MIME type is" && NetMime && NetTextResult into field "status"
end
```

NetLastModDate()

This function returns the "last modified date" string from an HTTP item called by GetNetText or PreLoadNetThing commands. The NetLastModDate function can only be called when the NetDone or NetError commands report that the operation is complete. Shockwave discards the results of the previous operation in order to conserve memory.

Syntax:

```
NetLastModDate ( text )
```

Example:

This example puts the last modified date into a field named "status."

```
on mousedown
  put NetLastModDate into field "status"
end
```

NetAbort

This command cancels a network operation without waiting for a result.

Syntax:

```
NetAbort ( ID )
```

Example:

This example cancels the previous network operation when the mouse is clicked.

```
on mousedown
 NetAbort
end
```

GetLatestNetID ()

It is possible to have more than one network operation active at a time. When you start two operations at the same time, Lingo needs a way to keep track of them during downloading. After one operation starts, and before the next operation begins, the GetLatestNetID function retrieves a unique identifier for that operation.

Syntax:

```
GetLatestNetID ( text )
```

Example 1:

This example returns the Net ID of an asynchronous operation just started into a field named "status."

```
on mousedown
 put GetLatestNetID into field "status"
end
```

Each of the functions NetDone, NetError, NetTextResult, NetMIME, NetLastModDate, and NetAbort allow an optional parameter specifying the unique identifier returned by GetLatestNetID.

Example 2:

This example gets the Net ID of an operation and then aborts that same operation. The X in this example is a local variable. It is used to pass the resulting string from the GetLatestNetID command to the NetAbort command.

```
on mousedown
 put GetLatestNetID into X
 NetAbort ( X )
end
```

Additional Lingo Examples and Ideas

This section is designed to give you ideas about old and new Lingo commands and ways that you can blend the two together for Shockwave. Where the CD icon is present, you will find an example movie on the CD.

The Time Command

This Lingo command returns the current time in the user's system clock. It can return the time in two formats: long and short.

Syntax:

```
The Short Time      "1:30 PM"
The Long Time       "1:30:24 PM"
```

Example:

Use this example to put a real-time clock (with the seconds) in your Shockwave movie. The following script needs to go in the movie script window, and you need a text field named "time" on the stage.

```
on idle
put (the long time) into field "time"
end
```

The Date Command

The date command can be used alone or with the time command to give you both the date and time.

Syntax:

```
The Short Date      "9/7/95"
The Long Date       "Saturday, September 7, 1995
```

Example:

This example needs to be in the movie script to work. It uses both the time and the date commands in a text file named "info."

```
on idle
put (the long date) && (the long time) into field "info"
end
```

Lingo Commands for Shockwave

Random HTTP Jumper

This example uses the "Random" Lingo command and the "GoToNetPage" function to randomly select between three different HTTP locations when clicked.

Syntax:

```
Random ( value )
```

Example:

```
on mousedown
put Random (3) into X
 if X=1 then GoToNetPage (" http://www.server1.com ")
 if X=2 then GoToNetPage (" http://www.server2.com ")
 if X=3 then GoToNetPage (" http://www.server3.com ")
end
```

ColorDepth Control

Using the Lingo color depth command, your Shockwave movie can either change the monitor color depth automatically or the user can click a button to switch color.

Syntax:

```
The ColorDepth
```

Example:

This example gets the color depth of the monitor and saves it into a global named "gMonitor." Then it sets the color depth to 8-bit, if it's not already set there. Finally, just before the movie ends, it sets the color depth back to the user's original setting. Both handlers go in the movie script.

```
on startmovie
global gMonitor
 put the colordepth into gMonitor
 if the colordepth <> 8 then set the colordepth to 8
end
on stopmovie
global gMonitor
 set the colordepth to gMonitor
end
```

SoundLevel Control

The SoundLevel command allows you to control the global volume setting of the user's machine. It would be a waste of time for you to incorporate sounds into your Shockwave movie only to find out that the volume on the user's machine is set to 0.

65

Syntax:

    The SoundLevel

Example:

This example gets the user's volume setting and saves it in a global called gVolume. It then sets the volume to 7. And lastly, just before the movie quits, it returns the volume to its original setting. Both handlers go in the movie script.

```
on startmovie
global gVolume
  put the soundlevel into gVolume
  if the soundlevel <> 7 then set the soundlevel to 7
end
on stopmovie
global gVolume
  set the soundlevel to gVolume
end
```

Custom Cursor in a Browser

Using the Cursor Lingo command, you can design a custom cursor in the Paint window and then switch the normal Internet browser cursor to your custom cursor. Your custom cursor cannot exceed 16×16 pixels, and it needs to be 1-bit. Or you can switch the cursor to a predefined system cursor.

Syntax:

    Cursor (CastNumber, MaskNumber)
    Cursor (WhichCursor)

The term *WhichCursor* must be a value from the table below:

(-1)	Arrow or pointer
(1)	I-beam cursor
(2)	Crosshair cursor
(3)	Crossbar cursor
(4)	Watch cursor
(200)	Blank (no) cursor

Example:

This example changes the cursor to a watch cursor until the PreLoadNetThing operation is completed. The completion of the PreLoadNetThing operation is reported by the NetDone command. This is a movie or Score script.

```
on idle
  if (NetDone) = FALSE then cursor (4)
  if (NetDone) = TRUE then cursor (-1)
end
```

Color 1-Bit Cast Members

After you dither a cast member to 1-bit (black and white), the black can be changed by the Lingo command "forecolor color of sprite" to any color in the 8-bit palette.

Syntax:

```
The ForeColor of Sprite ( WhichSprite ) to ( Color )
```

Example:

Changing the color of a sprite during a mouseDown is a useful way to indicate when the sprite is clicked. Be sure to use the updatestage command if your movie is running in one frame. This is a cast or Score script.

```
on mousedown
  set the forecolor of sprite 1 to 218
  updatestage
end
```

To pick a color, open the Palette window (Command-8) in Director. You can click on the color you like, and it will tell you the color number. You can also resize the Palette window to make a selection easier.

Tracking User Input

By using the Lingo command "LastEvent," you can see how long it's been since the user has moved the mouse, clicked the mouse, or pressed a key on the keyboard. This is good for a movie where users might need help in some way.

Syntax:

```
The LastEvent
```

Example:

This example watches the user's activity level and if nothing happens for 60 seconds, sends him to a different HTTP page or a marker in your movie. This is a movie or Score script.

```
on idle
  if (the LastEvent) > (60 * 60) then
    -- go marker "help" or
    GoToNetPage (" http://www.yourserver.com ")
  end if
-- This line is commented out. Remove the "--"
end
```

Disabled XObjects in Shockwave

In order to protect your user's local machine, XObjects are disabled in Shockwave. If XObjects worked inside of Shockwave, the security of the user's machine would be in question. XObjects allow you to read and write files to and from local hard drives. Not only is reading and writing a function of XObjects, but so is deleting a file or opening and closing the serial ports of the machine. Taking control of external devices, such as a CD-ROM drive, is also possible with XObjects. By removing these features, Macromedia felt that people would feel more comfortable with the new way of communicating on the Internet.

1. FileIO XObject

This XObject reads and writes text files that contain data, such as saved game data for a Director title, a list of names and addresses, or any type of data information, including pict files. This is a **disabled** feature in the Internet version of Shockwave.

2. SerialPort XObject

The SerialPort XObject can send and receive data through the serial port much like a modem. It can also make memory instances of any Lingo object and then control another Director movie via the serial port. This is a **disabled** feature in the Internet version of Shockwave.

3. OrthoPlay XObject

The OrthoPlay XObject has the capability to control external devices that play video or audio, such as a laserdisk player, a VCR, or an internal or external CD player. This is a **disabled** feature in Internet version of Shockwave.

Disabled Director-Related Commands

Since XObjects were omitted for control and security reasons, certain Lingo commands needed to also be disabled. The following is a list of disabled Director functions.

- ◆ Access to resource files and external libraries.
- ◆ MIAW (movies in a window).

- External linked media elements.
- Saving your Shockwave movie via Lingo.
- Printing from your Shockwave movie.

Number three, linked media, includes QuickTime movies. Because QuickTime is treated as an external linked file in Director, Shockwave doesn't support it. Yet.

1. Resource and XLib Commands

In order to disable access to external resources and libraries, the following Lingo commands do not function when your movie is playing back through the Shockwave Plug-In.

```
OpenXLib      CloseXLib
OpenResFile   CloseResFile
```

These Lingo commands control all access to external resource files located outside a Director movie. These are all **disabled** features in the Internet version of Shockwave.

2. Open Window and Close Window Commands

The MIAW feature in Director is disabled because it would cause windows to jump open outside the Internet browser. This causes "focus" conflicts between the MIAW windows and the browser window. The following Lingo commands have been removed to prevent MIAW access.

```
Open Window Dcx
Close Window
```

By disabling these Lingo commands, Shockwave automatically **disables** all MIAW-related Lingo commands as well.

3. ImportFileInto Command

Since Shockwave is running over the Internet, the use of externally linked media is **disabled**. These include linked graphics, sounds, and QuickTime files. There is only one Lingo command that allows the access of external linked media, the ImportFileInto command. This command does not function in Shockwave.

Just because this command is disabled does not mean that you cannot import linked media. Linked media works the same, however, just not in Shockwave. So make sure that when you are importing a cast member you don't have the "link to file" option enabled.

4. SaveMovie Command

When a Shockwave movie is transferred over the Internet to a user's browser, the movie is copied into the local cache file and then plays from there. Because Shockwave does not set up a link via the Internet to the original movie, the user is not allowed to save any changes to the Director movie. This broken link resulted in disabling the SaveMovie Lingo command from Shockwave.

5. PrintFrom Command

Macromedia considered leaving the printing function in Shockwave, however, printing is an external operation. And all external operations need to be deactivated in order to give users the feeling of security. If one external operation works, why not others? For this reason, the PrintFrom Lingo command was **disabled**.

The PrintFrom command prints whatever is displayed on the stage at a specific frame or range of frames.

Disabled System-Related Commands

Other sets of disabled commands that prevent Director movies from performing operations that could cause problems on the user's machine are listed below. By omitting these commands, users are protected from downloading Shockwave movies that contain viruses or can do other system-level damage. The disabled commands are as follows:

1. The Open command.
2. The Quit, Restart, and Shutdown commands.
3. The file location, path, and properties commands.
4. The MCI (Media Control Interface) command for windows.

1. Open

The Lingo Open command is used to open any external application from within Director. This is **disabled** in Shockwave in order to protect the user from getting viruses and causing other application damage.

2. Quit, Restart, and Shutdown Commands

The following system-specific Lingo commands are **disabled** in Shockwave: Quit, Restart, and ShutDown.

    Quit

The Quit command allows you to stop running your current movie.

    Restart

The Restart command will restart the user's machine by using your Director movie.

    ShutDown

The ShutDown command will close all open applications and then shut off the user's computer.

3. File Name, Path Properties, and Functions

Because control over linked media is not a feature of Shockwave, all the linked media commands and properties are **disabled**. Here is a list of the commands:

    FileName of cast
    FileName of window
    GetNthFileNameInFolder
    MoviePath
    PathName
    SearchCurrentFolder
    SearchPath

All these commands allow linking to external files, windows, or paths, and they do not function in Shockwave.

4. MCI Command

The media control interface used in Windows falls under the category of device control and is therefore **disabled** in Shockwave.

The following Lingo command is omitted from Shockwave:

    MCI (*command*)

The MCI command passes strings to the Windows media control interface, such as play, stop, or pause. This command is used for controlling everything from CD-ROM drives to MPEG video boards.

Macromedia Developer Profile

Name: Bruce Hunt
Title: Director of Networked Players

How did you get involved on the Shockwave team?

Norm M. hired me to run Director 6 and Networked Players. Shockwave is the core of the Network Players group.

What is your greatest contribution to Shockwave?

I managed to get the Shockwave Distribution Center built and the release process built for it while attempting to remain friends with the Web team.

What is the coolest thing about Shockwave?

The incredibly talented and fun-to-work-with Shockwave Engineering and QA Teams.

What is the "uncoolest" thing about Shockwave?

I wish our external development partner cared as much about the quality of their product as the Shockwave Product Team cares about it.

What is the one thing you would change in Shockwave if you had enough time?

The EMBED Tag would work right. More kinds of compression for media types would be available. Oops, that's two.

What is your favorite Shockwave Easter egg?

I'll never tell!

What one word (other than "shocking") describes your experience with Shockwave?

Exhilarating!

What one statement typifies your experiences during the Shockwave product cycle?

"Wow, Cool!"

How long have you been at Macromedia?

Six months.

Where were you working before?

SilverFox Technology, Inc.

What did you do?

Vice President of Engineering.

One interesting fact about you?

I co-authored the (now classic) performance paper on Ethernet and introduced the term, "CSMA-CD." I have a patent on building efficient Local Area Networks based on collision detection. I led the project that created Hallmark's TouchScreen Greetings Kiosks. I built a mil-spec Macintosh for Apple.

Your greatest accomplishment?

I have a great family.

What are the longest number of continuous hours you have worked at Macromedia?

18 hours.

What's the worst Shockwave tagline you have heard?

That's nothing but shockware!

What is the longest wait you've had for a download?

30 minutes.

Was it worth it?

No!

How many hours do you surf per day?

30 minutes.

Chapter 6

Using Afterburner— Post Processor for Director

Afterburner is the final step in your Shockwave movie creation process. The application has no interface, and is therefore foolproof to use. This is the simplest part of using Shockwave. You start the application like any other, by double-clicking it. In the current version you will not see a start-up screen, just menu items. The simplest method of compression is through the drag-and-drop method. You can drag the icon of your finished Director movie to the icon of the Afterburner application, and it will automatically open, compress, and rename the file for you. The file name will become the name of your Director movie plus the DCR file extension. During the compression, Afterburner will display a dialog box that indicates the estimated progress of the current movie. When this is done, your movie has been successfully compressed.

The current compression ratio can range from 40 to 60 percent of the original file size. The 20 percent variation comes from the use of sounds in your Director movie. Afterburner currently cannot compress audio samples that are in your movie(s).

Optimal Compression Techniques for "Burning" Your Movies

To help optimize the compression of your Director movie you should double-check the following things in your movie.

- ◆ All your cast members are at or below 8-bit color.
- ◆ All your audio samples have been cropped and downsampled.
- ◆ 1-bit cast members are used when single color cast members are needed.
- ◆ All redundant colors have been deleted from cast members.

- Any unused cast members have been deleted.
- You have saved and compressed your movie from Director.

At this point Afterburner can compress your movies to their fullest. Afterburner uses built-in compression techniques not unlike the JPEG or GIF compression schemes to reduce and remove redundant color and data.

The Insider's Perspective

How do you explain the differences between Shockwave and Java?

Bruce Hunt: Shockwave leverages the 10 years of Director development by Macromedia. No one knows more about how to create great multimedia development tools than Macromedia. We have spent years understanding how to integrate media items and present them rapidly on the screen and provide the highest quality sound. We have had the help of literally hundreds of thousands of multimedia developers who have guided the development of the tools. The result is tools that are optimized to provide the best media integration in the business.

Java is a programming language designed principally to be cross platform. Its tools for media integration, management, and animation are primitive compared to Director. To be sure, talented programmers with sufficient time and customer experience could re-create many of the capabilities found in Director, but hardly in time to get a multimedia production published.

The principle difference is in the level of the tool set. Director is designed as a set of tools targeted at creating multimedia titles; Java is a general programming language out of which tools such as Director's could be created. So the difference is in the amount of time that a developer is willing to invest and the level of knowledge that a developer must attain to create multimedia titles in either Java or Shockwave.

Shockwave is a higher level tool that is dramatically easier to develop multimedia titles in; Java isn't designed as a multimedia toolkit. In fact, Macromedia has signed up to create a set of multimedia classes for Java and to make sure that Java Applets can run as Director Xtras. In short, we are going to assist in providing a set of tools so that Java can begin to attain the multimedia capabilities of Shockwave for Director.

Harry Chesley: Director/Shockwave is a multimedia authoring environment and delivery system. Java is a general-purpose programming language.

Chris Walcott: Shockwave has a user interface (Director). Java is a C-like language.

Sarah Allen: I haven't used Java yet, but from everything I hear, I think I'll like it. I like programming languages, but when I want to write a letter, I use a word processor, not a programming language. Shockwave isn't a programming language. If I wanted to develop a Web experience with lots of moving graphics, whizzy transitions, sound, and interactivity, I'd use Shockwave. If I wanted to create a Web site that does something that Director cannot do, I might use Java.

John Newlin: I'm not sure I understand what you want here, but here goes... Shockwave has a very fast animation engine that can composite 48 sprites on the screen using different ink modes, stretching, shrinking, and play up to eight mixed channels of sound all in real time. It is the premier multimedia authoring tool. Java, on the other hand, can do simple animations, but its strong point is that it is a very portable language with some nice features built in. These include security, small run-time size, fast interpreter, and a portable set of classes. If you write a Java application, it will run on any host that has an interpreter. I guess the same is true for Shockwave.

Sherri Sheridan: Shockwave is just doing Director, and Java requires C programming.

Ken Day: Director is more efficient for the developer and a very rich development environment. Java is perfect for developing performance-critical elements, but requires more of a programmer than Director. Director is accessible to a much wider range of graphic artists.

Current Compression

The current compression technique used by the Afterburner application is similar to the compression algorithms found in graphic file formats. Because your Director movie is comprised of mostly graphical data, this compression technique is best. The compression scheme looks at your cast members pixel by pixel to determine if redundant color is used anywhere. Shockwave makes a note of this redundant color and continues to check and compress the file.

The current compressor only works on graphical data. The compressor is not used on any audio data installed in your movie. This will change in future versions of Shockwave.

Customized Compression Techniques

You may have noticed that your Afterburner application came with an empty folder called "Xtras." This folder is for future compressors that Shockwave will support. The Xtra compressors can be developed by anyone for any type of media element, such as audio or QuickTime. If you are interested in developing or finding a developer for Xtras, you can contact Macromedia's registered developer group at the corporate headquarters office in San Francisco. The current development language for the Xtra's kit is C++.

The Macromedia developer program's group will not only keep you current on all the latest developments with Shockwave, but will also help you find other Shockwave developers and user groups in your local area. Check them out.

Fried Green Director Movies: The Afterburner Scoop

Why call the compressor "Afterburner?"

Bruce Hunt: Well, we could call it Beforeburner.

Harry Chesley: Afterburner burns off all the excess stuff and compresses the movie, thereby accelerating it across the network....

John Newlin: Why not?

Sherri Sheridan: Ask Ken.

Ken Day: Afterburner just made sense with Shockwave. We tried a few things related to movies, like cutting a print, but didn't come up with anything quite so flashy. I'm still a little bummed we no longer have Afterburner producing Fried Green Director Movies, but at least the Mac file type is still FGDM. But even at the time I knew our backroom humor couldn't last.

Who thought of the name "Afterburner?"

BH: I don't know.

HC: I did. I don't remember any details. We thought about it for a few days—I believe it was just me and Ken Day at that point—and Afterburner was the best one. We tried some other movie-related things, but nothing very good and nothing I remember. Ken may remember more.

JN: Ken Day, or Harry I think.

SS: I think Ken and Harry.

KD: Me.

What would you have rather named it?

BH: CompressionWave.

HC: Nothing.

JN: No idea.

SS: I love the name; it's perfect.

KD: Afterburner.

Chapter 7

Adding Multimedia to Your Web Site

This section will cover the principles of adding new HTML tags, such as <EMBED> and <NOEMBED>, to your Web pages in order to incorporate Shockwave movies. In addition, you will learn how to optimize your Shockwave-enhanced pages for as many Web browsers as possible.

"Smart" HTML Authoring for Shockwave

Now that you've learned how to create your own Shockwave movies in Director and compress them with Afterburner, you're ready to add them to your Web site. There are two ways to go about adding multimedia to your Web site—the smart way and the not-so-smart way. And because you bought this book (the first step in the right direction!), let's assume you want to learn the smarter way. This "smart HTML authoring" means that you must take into consideration all the possible scenarios your Web end users might experience—everything from the page's download time to how their PC will mix multiple movie sounds. This awareness will translate into a Shockwave Web site that your end users will want to visit over and over again (see Figure 7.1).

Macromedia Shockwave for Director

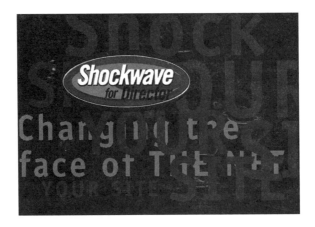

Figure 7.1 *The Shockwave home page.*

In Chapter 4 you found that you can use most of the existing Director features to produce your Shockwave files with a few new twists. And likewise, you will find you can use most of the existing HTML tags that currently exist to build your Shockwave Web pages, as well as a few new ones (see Figure 7.2). Currently, the user can interact with the movie and enter text from the keyboard into text fields programmed into the movie, or scroll through a Web page containing a movie while the movie is playing in the page. The movie itself, using new HTML and Lingo commands, can access information from the network and open additional URLs in the browser window.

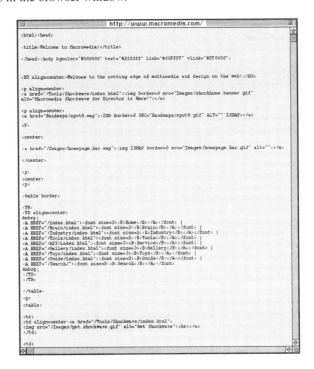

Figure 7.2 *The Macromedia home page.*

Adding Multimedia to Your Web Site

You can easily enhance your Web site with Shockwave by adding files to your server and the new HTML to your page. But before we begin, there are some items you may want to take into consideration while authoring your HTML pages:

- Overall page sizes and download times
- Multiple movies on a page
- Sounds in multiple movies
- Looping movies

Overall Page Sizes and Download Times

One of the most significant, yet often overlooked, aspects of HTML page creation is the overall page "size" and download time associated with it. The "overall size" means the total kilobytes of all the GIFs, JPEGs, text, and Shockwave movies on each page. It is critical that Web site producers take this overall size issue into consideration when authoring any HTML pages, but it's particularly important when including any rich media type, such as Shockwave.

Today, sizes of pages delivered over the Internet should be carefully reviewed primarily because many users dial in at relatively slow connection speeds—9,600 and 14,400 bits per second. At these rates, the user sees only about 1 KB per second of effective throughput. If the Internet host is heavily loaded or there's network traffic congestion, the rate can drop even lower. See the *Download Times* chart in Chapter 3 for more details.

Smart Authoring Tips

- Let the user choose from Shockwave pages with different file sizes and include estimated download times for different connection speeds.
- Make the Shockwave movie download optional on a page.
- Allow the user to turn the sound on/off in a Shockwave movie.
- Always consider if there is any way to reduce the size of the page and movie to shorten the user's download wait time.
- Allow a user to control the start/stop of an animation.
- On each HTML page, use only one Shockwave movie with sound.
- Always program a looped Shockwave movie to stop playing after a given amount of time.

Although technically there's no limit to how many movies you can incorporate into a Web page or how large the individual movie file size may be, it is wise to point out that your audience's patience *is* limited and should be considered carefully when coordinating a Shockwave Web page.

Does your content justify a longer download time? Sometimes an interactive game or tutorial will be worth the user's wait. Some people have tried to set specific limits for page sizes and download times, but we believe that the content and connection speeds can vary to such a degree that it is best to use your common sense, always do user testing, and listen to your audience's feedback.

Multiple Movies on a Page

When you have more than one Shockwave file on a page, each movie uses an additional amount of RAM (approximately 50 to 100K) over and above the actual movie file size. Users with limited RAM may have problems viewing pages with several Shockwave movies. However, when the user goes to another page, Shockwave frees the RAM it no longer needs to display movies.

Sounds in Multiple Movies

With certain sound cards in Windows 3.1 or Windows 95, you might find technical problems when the browser tries to sort out the sound tracks of two movies playing simultaneously. However, if you carefully design the sound sources for your multiple movie Web pages, this won't be a problem. In some cases, you can even enable the user to interactively turn short sounds on and off on pages with multiple movies.

Looping Movies

Movies programmed to loop indefinitely tie up the processor and can cause problems, distractions, and frustration for the user. You should always set your looping movie to stop after a certain period of time or enable the user to control the start and stop of the loop with a click of the mouse.

Writing HTML for Shockwave

Writing HTML for Web pages that contain Shockwave movies is not any different than writing regular Web pages. It still consists of simple text editing, with a few new HTML tags added like <EMBED> and <NOEMBED>. When you use the new <EMBED> command, the movie is called and plays right within your page. The <NOEMBED> command acts like an "alt" or "alternate" tag for browsers that do not have the Shockwave Plug-In installed.

Netscape 2.0 Browser

To view the Shockwave movies, users need to have Netscape Navigator 2.0 for Windows or Macintosh with the appropriate Shockwave Plug-In. The Netscape Navigator 2.0 version can be downloaded from Netscape's home page:

```
http://home.netscape.com/
```

Installation instructions for the Shockwave Plug-In can be found on Macromedia's Web site:

```
http://www.macromedia.com/
```

The new <EMBED> tag

The <EMBED> tag is recognized by Netscape Navigator 2.0 and other forthcoming browsers to indicate an area on the Web page that will contain special embedded content. Browsers that recognize <EMBED> properly will use the Shockwave Plug-In to interpret the information specified by the SRC parameter. Here is the basic syntax for the <EMBED> tag:

```
<EMBED SRC="myfile" WIDTH=x HEIGHT=y>
```

When you want to use the <EMBED> tag to add a Shockwave for Director movie to an HTML page, you can substitute the stage's height in pixels for y, the stage's width in pixels for x, and the filename or URL in quotes after SRC.

```
<EMBED SRC="directory path/myfile.dcr" WIDTH=x HEIGHT=y>
```

Make sure that the width and height are the same as the stage size of the Director movie in pixels. You can find this Stage Size information in Director under the File menu under Preferences. This step is very important because Netscape will crop the Shockwave area to the size you specify.

The new <NOEMBED> tag

If the user's browser doesn't support the Shockwave Plug-In, the <NOEMBED> tag enables you to substitute a JPEG or GIF image in place of the movie, acting like the familiar alternate text indicator in the IMG SRC tag.

    <NOEMBED> <IMG SRC="directory path/myfile.gif"> </NOEMBED>

You can substitute any HTML source—that is, text, linked text, GIF, or JPEG—for a shocked movie in the syntax of the NOEMBED command.

The new TEXTFOCUS argument (optional)

You can use the optional TEXTFOCUS argument to tell the Shockwave movie when to start responding to input from the keyboard. The values for TEXTFOCUS are described in the following table. If you don't include the TEXTFOCUS argument, Shockwave uses the default onMouse setting.

    onMouse:

The Shockwave movie begins responding to input from the keyboard after the user clicks anywhere on the movie with the mouse. This is the default setting for all Shockwave movies.

    onStart:

The Shockwave movie begins responding to input from the keyboard as soon as the movie starts running.

    never:

The Shockwave movie ignores all input from the keyboard.

HTML for Netscape 2.0

Here's an example that shows how to set up the <EMBED> and <NOEMBED> tags for a compressed Director movie named "shockmovie.dcr" that is 400 pixels wide by 300 pixels high and responds to input from the keyboard as soon as it starts running:

    <EMBED SRC="http://www.yourserver.com/movies/shockmovie.dcr" WIDTH=400
    HEIGHT=300 TEXTFOCUS=onStart>

HTML for All Other Browsers

If you come across a Web page that contains an HTML tag that your browser doesn't understand, your browser will simply ignore the tag. This is standard behavior for Web browsers, guaranteeing that future improvements in the HTML standard won't force you to pick up new browser software. The only problem with this scheme is in the case of an old browser recognizing an HTML tag whose meaning has changed since the old browser was released.

This is precisely the case with Netscape Navigator 1.1N and the <EMBED> tag. Due to an improvement in the HTML standard, Netscape Navigator 2.0 recognizes the <EMBED> tag as indicating content that must be processed by a plug-in. Navigator 1.1N also recognizes <EMBED>, but it interprets the tag as specifying an OLE link (supporting the Windows 3.1 object linking and embedding model). Consequently, when someone using Navigator 1.1N comes across an <EMBED> tag indicating a Shockwave movie, Navigator 1.1N will display *the dreaded broken icon*.

Avoiding the broken icon

There is a workaround for avoiding every Webmaster's nightmare: the infamous broken icon. What causes broken icons? You will see a broken icon on a Web page if its HTML makes reference to a source file that cannot be located or downloaded, which happens frequently to graphics when their links change. In older versions of Netscape—Netscape 1.1N and on other browsers—the user will see a broken image icon in addition to the substitute image even using the <EMBED> and <NOEMBED> tag scenario shown above.

The solution—a JavaScript™ workaround

Netscape's JavaScript (formerly known as LiveScript) can be used to eliminate the broken image icon in some situations for the Netscape Navigator 2.0 browsers:

- ◆ Reveal the <EMBED> tag, so a Shockwave movie will appear if the Plug-In is loaded; if the Plug-In isn't loaded, a broken icon will appear and direct the user to the download area or possibly download the appropriate plug-in automatically.
- ◆ Hide the <NOEMBED> block, so the consolation HTML text or graphic will not appear.

Macromedia Shockwave for Director

For all browsers earlier or other than Netscape Navigator 2.0, try the following:

- ◆ Hide the <EMBED> tag, so the Shockwave movie will not appear.
- ◆ Reveal the <NOEMBED> block, so the consolation HTML text or graphic will appear.

Let's say that you want a GIF image called "getshockwave.gif" (whose dimensions are 125 × 68 pixels) to appear as a consolation to people who don't have Navigator 2.0. For those people who do have Navigator 2.0, you want the page to load a Shockwave movie named "shockmovie.dcr" (whose stage dimensions are 320 × 120). To have something appear in place of the Shockwave movie if the user has another browser, you can use a pair of HTML tags understood only by Navigator 2.0, <NOEMBED> and </NOEMBED>. When Navigator 2.0 encounters a <NOEMBED> tag, it ignores everything from that point until it reaches the </NOEMBED> tag. Other browsers, which do not understand <NOEMBED> and </NOEMBED>, will ignore both of them and execute the HTML between those tags.

```
<SCRIPT LANGUAGE="JavaScript">
<!-- Hide this script from non-Navigator 2.0 browsers.
 document.write( '<EMBED SRC="shockmovie.dcr" WIDTH=320 HEIGHT=120>' );
<!-- Done hiding from non-Navigator 2.0 browsers. -->
</SCRIPT>
<NOEMBED>
<IMG SRC="getshockwave.gif" WIDTH=125 HEIGHT=68>
</NOEMBED>
```

Adding Multimedia to Your Web Site

How JavaScript works

If you load this HTML with Netscape Navigator 2.0, it will encounter the JavaScript routine and execute it. If the Shockwave Plug-In is installed, the movie will appear. If the Plug-In is absent, then a broken icon will appear. Then, when Navigator 2.0 sees the <NOEMBED> tag, it skips over everything between it and </NOEMBED>. So the image "getshockwave.gif" will not appear.

If you load this HTML with any other browser, it will encounter the JavaScript routine and ignore it, thinking that it's just a comment. Then it will see the <NOEMBED> tag and ignore that as well, because it doesn't recognize that either. Consequently, it will display the image "getshockwave.gif" because only Navigator 2.0 knows to skip over anything between <NOEMBED> and </NOEMBED>.

```
<SCRIPT LANGUAGE="JavaScript">
<!-- Hide this script from non-Navigator 2.0 browsers.
 document.write( '<EMBED SRC="shockmovie.dcr" WIDTH=320 HEIGHT=120>' );
<!-- Done hiding from non-Navigator 2.0 browsers. -->
</SCRIPT>
```

Only Navigator 2.0 can interpret this JavaScript routine because it's hidden inside a pair of comment tags, <!-- and -->. Anything in an HTML document between these tags is ignored, except in the special case of Navigator 2.0 and JavaScript. For this reason, do not remove the comments, as they are necessary for the functioning of this script. You should notice that the first line after the <SCRIPT ... > tag begins with an open comment tag (<!--), but also that this line doesn't contain a close comment (-->) tag. Instead, the comment is concluded on the last line before the </SCRIPT> tag. If you close the comment on the first line, then this routine will fail. Avoid the crash—use WIDTH and HEIGHT with your <IMG ... > tags. If you have images on your Web page, be sure to specify their WIDTH and HEIGHT values.

By hiding the <EMBED> tag from Netscape Navigator 1.1N, we have prevented that browser from displaying a broken icon. However, the Shockwave Plug-In is required for Navigator 2.0 to avoid the broken icon. Overall, this solution works great with Navigator 2.0 and all other existing browsers (including Navigator 1.1N). Upcoming browsers will properly interpret <EMBED> and won't see the tag unless they also understand JavaScript.

Macromedia Developer Profile

Name: Sherri Sheridan
Title: Shockwave Artist/Engineer

How did you get involved on the Shockwave team?

I knew it was going to make history.

What is your greatest contribution to Shockwave?

Teaching people how to make Shockwave movies and being psychically connected to the code during testing so I knew which areas were buggy and cut the QA process to a fraction of the time.

In your opinion, what is the coolest thing about Shockwave?

PreloadNetThing.

In your opinion, what is the "uncoolest" thing about Shockwave?

Lack of a Paco player type compressor for video clips.

Adding Multimedia to Your Web Site

What is the one thing you would change in Shockwave if you had enough time?

The capability to have users interact in real time in Shockwave movies on Web pages like World Chat. I've been bugging Harry for this, and he says he's working on doing it with GetNetText.

What is your favorite Shockwave Easter egg?

Ummm... the solid gold ones.

What one word (other than "shocking") describes your experience with Shockwave?

Futureshock.

What one statement typifies your experiences during the Shockwave product cycle?

"Sleep is for the weak."

How long have you been at Macromedia?

Since July '95.

Where were you working before?

I have my own company with six other people called Mind's Eye Media.

What did you do?

3D Animation and Digital Video special FX for money, but I was actually in the process of creating the first independent feature film edited solely on the Macintosh but my hard drives kept dying from the file sizes so I decided to try something less stressful for awhile.

One interesting fact about you?

I'm also writing a book on Shockwave due out about the same time. *(Cool!-Ed.)*

Your greatest accomplishment?

Traveling around the world three times in two years as a buyer for an import/export company after graduating from college and hitting almost every continent while missing only a few countries in the process. It cured my wanderlust and filled me with lots of wisdom and interesting stories. My favorite country is India because it's like being in a third-world Fellini film.

What are the longest number of continuous hours you have worked at Macromedia?

I try not to think about that day and night and day again...

What's the worst Shockwave tagline you have heard?

I have a policy to only remember good things fed to me from the media.

What is the longest wait you've had for a download? Was it worth it?

I always use Macromedia's T3 for the big downloads.

How many hours do you surf per day?

1–18 depending on when my eyes go blurry and how Shockwave's behaving that code version.

Macromedia Developer Profile

Name: Ken Day
Title: Senior Architect

How did you get involved on the Shockwave team?

I was hired for ITV. Harry and I noticed that what I was doing and what he was doing were VERY similar. I joined him for "a while" to develop "shared" technology.... Then the Web blew open, and I was here to stay. Now I expect some of the technology I expected to do for ITV to happen in Shockwave.

What is your greatest contribution to Shockwave?

The file structure is my design and my implementation. I'm proud of it.

In your opinion, what is the coolest thing about Shockwave?

It enables authors.

In your opinion, what is the "uncoolest" thing about Shockwave?

All the stuff we haven't gotten to... better integration of the authoring environment with Director, more compression, streaming.... Of those, probably the lack of streaming—you have to wait for the whole movie to download before you see anything.

How long have you been at Macromedia?

I joined at the beginning of last April.

Where were you working before?

Borland.

What did you do?

In my last life, I worked on PC database systems—several versions of Paradox, a couple of others. I did a lot of things in those systems, but my focus was organizing data on disk.

Chapter 8

Shockwave and Your Web Server

After having learned how to write proper HTML for Shockwave Web pages, you need to understand the best way to add them to your Web site. This section will show you how to upload your Shockwave files properly and set the mime types on your server to accommodate the new Shockwave DCR, DIR, and DXR file extensions.

Uploading Your Files Properly

First, you need to have completed your Director movie and Afterburned the file for optimal download times. Then using FTP software like Fetch, you can add the files to your site (see Figure 8.1).

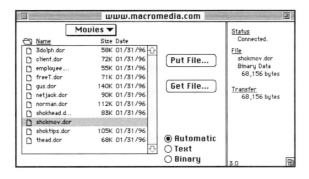

Figure 8.1 *Adding the files to your site.*

File Transfer Protocol

Using file transfer protocol (FTP) software, you can open the shortcut that you set up previously for your Web server, and the FTP software will connect you to it. Then select or create the proper directory for your Shockwave movie on the server (see Figure 8.2). Now "put" the Shockwave file on the server, with Binary Raw Data selected as the method for transferring the file. The Shockwave DCR file should then appear on your Web server and also appear in the HTML pages you have authored it into.

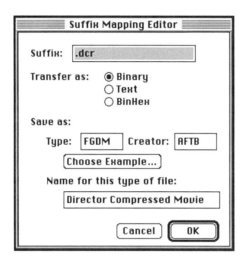

Figure 8.2 *Creating the correct extension for your file.*

Binary Raw Data

It is critical to add the file to the Web site as a binary (not text) file and as Raw Data (see Figure 8.3), as opposed to MacBinaryII or BinHex file. If the file is not uploaded as a binary Raw Data file, the Shockwave file will not display properly.

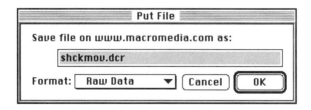

Figure 8.3 *All Shockwave files should be set to Raw Data.*

The Insider's Perspective

Why call the files "DCR"?

Bruce Hunt: Marketing wouldn't let us call them FGD for Fried Green Director! It came from DXR with the "C" standing for "Compression."

Harry Chesley: Marketing insisted on something starting with "D" and ending with "R."

Chris Walcott: Marketing said we had to. Marketing said it had to be "D<something>R."

Sarah Allen: "C" is for compressed, and all the other director file formats are D_R, like DIR, DXR; of course, I like to think that the "C" is for "Chesley," the founder of the team.

John Newlin: We had to name the file "D<something>R," and we could pick anything for the second letter. The "C" stands for "Compressed."

Sherri Sheridan: Long story—not that interesting either.

Ken Day: Director files are "D<something>R." "C" is for "Compressed."

What would you have rather named it?

BH: FGD

HC: FGD, for Fried Green Director movies. We did name them this, but marketing made us change it. I'm pretty sure it was John Newlin who said it in a meeting, just off-hand, and I grabbed it and started calling afterburned movies "fried green movies." The icon for fried movies is still a green frying pan with a movie strip in it (don't tell marketing).

SA: We had originally called them "fgd" files for fried green director movies. I never really expected that to get released, but it was fun while it lasted.

JN: FGD. FGD stands for Fried Green Director movies. We were sitting in a meeting talking about how Afterburner would fry a movie and the "cooked movie" would be delivered. And the phrase just popped out of my mouth, the "Fried Green Director Movie." In fact if you look at the Mac TYPE/CREATOR information, the TYPE is FGDM.

SS: DZR. Sounds animated—sorta spinning and woozy.

KD: They were originally FGD—the Fried line—but that couldn't last. These things need to make sense and be cohesive across a product. (I'm a little

surprised, and sort of happy, that the Mac file type has remained FGDM.) Oh, and about the movie: Yes, it was a reference to the (*Fried Green Tomatoes*) movie. It sounded quirky, was slightly intellectual, had NOTHING to do with computers or technology, and had a reference to burning (which an afterburner has to be able to do). It was just too obscure a connection NOT to use. But I wouldn't want to eat green tomatoes fried by an afterburner—too much gas smell.

Setting Mime Types on Your Server

Your HTTP server must be configured to recognize and handle Shockwave movies. Most servers are UNIX-based platforms, although there are also servers that use Mac HTTP or WebSTAR software. Just follow the directions provided here for the type of Web server you have. Luckily, this Shockwave mime type setup only needs to be done once and then never needs to be changed again.

UNIX Servers

You can configure your server yourself or have the system administrator do it for you.

To have your system administrator configure it, have him/her create an entry in the file that registers mime types. The administrator will need the following information:

- Mime type: application
- Sub Type: x-director
- Extensions: DCR, DIR, DXR

If you want to set the mime type yourself, create a file called ".htaccess." Check with your system administrator for the filename conventions at your site if this doesn't work.

Set file access permission to:

```
user = read and write
group = read
world = read
```

Set the file privileges to world readable by typing:

```
chmod 644 .htaccess
```

Place the file at the root level of your Web pages (such as the "public_html" directory). The file should contain the following line:

```
AddType application/x-director dcr
AddType application/x-director dir
AddType application/x-director dxr
```

Mac HTTP Servers

If you are running a Macintosh-based HTTP server, you need to modify the file "MacHTTP.config." Add the following lines to the file:

```
BINARY .DIR TEXT * application/x-director
BINARY .DXR TEXT * application/x-director
BINARY .DCR TEXT * application/x-director
```

WebSTAR Server

If you are using WebSTAR and would like to configure it to serve Shockwave movies, follow these directions:

1. Run the application called WebSTAR Admin.
2. Locate and select your server in the Pick A Server window (your server must be running).
3. Choose Suffix Mapping from the Configure menu. The Suffix Mapping dialog box appears.
4. Choose the following settings:

```
Action: BINARY
File Suffix: .DCR
File Type: TEXT
Creator: *
MIME Type: application/x-director
```

If you are providing DIR or DXR movies, repeat the process for each suffix you want to add.

After your Web server is configured for the Shockwave mime type and you have uploaded your Shockwave movies and Web pages to your Web server, all your hard work is about to pay off—you are now completely ready to experience Shockwave for Director on your own Web pages! Congratulations!

Macromedia Developer Profile

Name: John Newlin
Title: I don't need no stinkin' title <!>

How did you get involved on the Shockwave team?

Harry asked me if I wanted to move from the Director 5 team to work on Shockwave.

What is your greatest contribution to Shockwave?

I think the coolest thing I did was getting that original demo working for Digital World back in June 1995. Look what I started. :-)

In your opinion, what is the coolest thing about Shockwave?

The momentum that it is gaining in the marketplace. It's really cool to see all of these news articles about how great Shockwave is, and how it's changing the Web.

In your opinion, what is the uncoolest thing about Shockwave?

All of the bandwidth that downloading these movies takes. The Information Superhighway is in need of a few more lanes now :-)

What is the one thing you would change in Shockwave if you had enough time?

Add streaming support, so that a movie can start playing before it is completely downloaded.

What is your favorite Shockwave Easter egg?

Easter egg, what Easter eggs? There's only one that I know of, and that is our initials are on the wallpaper that is displayed before a movie plays.

What one word (other than "shocking") describes your experience with Shockwave?

Stress.

What one statement typifies your experiences during the Shockwave product cycle?

"It looks like Netscape did it to us again."

How long have you been at Macromedia?

Just over a year.

Where were you working before?

Lexmark International.

What did you do?

Worked on network code that allowed remote programmability of printers on a LAN.

One interesting fact about you?

There is nothing interesting about me. I'm completely boring. ;-)

Your greatest accomplishment?

Fixing all of those bugs in the Netscape browser so that our Shockwave Plug-In would work.

What are the longest number of continuous hours you have worked at Macromedia?

20

What is the longest wait you've had for a download? Was it worth it?

I'm a pretty impatient person—if something isn't downloading very fast, I kill the transfer and try again in the middle of the night when more bandwidth is available. :-)

How many hours do you surf per day?

1-2

Macromedia Developer Profile

Name: Chris Walcott
Title: QA Entomologist & Drum Master

How did you get involved on the Shockwave team?

Brought in by Sarah Allen.

What is your greatest contribution to Shockwave?

Finding bugs.

In your opinion, what is the coolest thing about Shockwave?

Bringing interactivity to the Web.

In your opinion, what is the "uncoolest" thing about Shockwave?

Big movies take a long time to download.

What is the one thing you would change in Shockwave if you had enough time?

Streaming files.

What is your favorite Shockwave Easter egg?

I could tell you, but then I'd have to kill you.

What one word (other than "shocking") describes your experience with Shockwave?

Fun.

What one statement typifies your experiences during the Shockwave product cycle?

"Who's staying for dinner?"

How long have you been at Macromedia?

6 months.

Where were you working before?

Adobe.

What did you do?

QA for Screen Ready.

One interesting fact about you?

I have a recording studio in my house.

Your greatest accomplishment?

Playing at the Filmore Auditorium with my band Code of the West.

What are the longest number of continuous hours you have worked at Macromedia?

Can't remember.

What's the worst Shockwave tagline you have heard?

"I've been shock'n all night, dude."

What is the longest wait you've had for a download? Was it worth it?

I have a T3 line here. Waiting is not an issue.

How many hours do you surf per day?

Not as much as you'd think. Too much work to do.

Chapter 9

Tips and Techniques from Real-World Shockwave Developers

This chapter gives you an opportunity to get inside the minds of top developers who work with Shockwave every day! You'll learn how to create an interactive corporate advertisement from scratch, make a realistic carnival game, play dress-up in The Spot, reinvent classic arcade games like Tetris and Asteroids, create an online musical experience for Sony Music, build an interactive educational Web site, generate complex "algorithmic animations" for high-impact visuals, and make cartoon parodies of entertainment industry advertising.

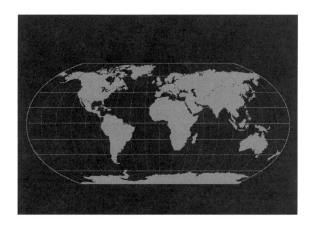

2-Lane Media

Goal: To make a realistic carnival game; play dress-up in The Spot.
Address: 1575 Westwood Blvd., Suite 301
Phone: 310-473-3706
Fax: 310-473-6736
Email: `tlanemedia@aol.com`
Web Site URL: `http://www.2-lanemedia.com/`

About 2-Lane Media

2-Lane Media is an Interactive Advertising and Marketing company located in Los Angeles, specializing in leveraging new media technologies to achieve quantifiable results. As an industry leader since 1993, 2-Lane Media has produced interactive marketing productions for such clients as Disney, Paramount Pictures, Prudential Securities, Edelman Public Relations, Ketchum Communications Worldwide, Columbia TriStar, DC Comics, Virgin Records, and Warner*Active*. Additionally, 2-Lane Media was awarded the first CLIO in the newly recognized Interactive Advertising category in 1995 and has received over 17 industry awards or finalist nominations in the past three years.

Company Focus

2-Lane Media has concentrated its efforts on interactive marketing and advertising. The company has excelled at maximizing the features of Macromedia Director to produce award-winning Director productions for both CD-ROM and floppy disk. 2-Lane is also one of the top World Wide Web site producers in the country, having completed work on several high-profile sites. We provide integrated interactive solutions for both the business-to-business and consumer markets, utilizing multiple platforms and delivery methods. Our specialties include producing everything from floppy-sized Interactive Press Kits (IPKs) and demos to CD-ROMs, kiosks, laptop sales tools, and Web sites. We recently completed work on the critically acclaimed high-traffic Web site for the blockbuster Disney film, *Toy Story* (`www.toystory.com`).

Clients and Projects

2-Lane Media has produced interactive marketing and advertising for a who's who list of top corporate, advertising, and entertainment companies. Among them, 2-Lane produced a series of Interactive Floppy Disk Press Kits for the major motion picture studios and Hollywood On-line. These include press kits for *Forrest Gump, The Mask, Addams Family Values*, and *Naked Gun 33 1/3*. 2-Lane Media has also produced floppy disk Interactive Press Kits for Boy George's album *Cheapness and Beauty* for Virgin Records, for DC Comics' release of their new comic book series *Sovereign Seven*, and for two CD-ROM games published by Warner*Active*, entitled *Panic In The Park* and *Where's Waldo At The Circus?* 2-Lane Media has produced CD-ROM brochures/catalogs and CD and laptop-based sales presentations for the likes of Prudential Securities, Edelman Public Relations, Sanyo Mobile Audio, The Western Cable Show, and others. On the Internet, some of the Web sites that 2-Lane has produced or coproduced include the *Toy Story* site for Disney, the Web site for Columbia/Tristar's film release *First Knight,* and the Web site for Oakwood Corporate Housing, as well as home pages for some other smaller companies. We have also created other interactive demos, tutorials, and kiosk projects on various platforms ranging from floppies to 3DO, CD-I, and LANs.

Impact of the Internet

As an Interactive Marketing and Advertising agency that offers complete solutions for clients, the Internet has become a major portion of 2-Lane Media's focus. The majority of the requests that clients have asked for since 1995 involve World Wide Web sites in addition to or in place of other interactive media. Some clients merely want a basic Web presence while others want to create a major marketing or commerce-driven site. To support this burgeoning new industry focus, 2-Lane Media has hired Web markup specialists and programmers and has turned its own creative direction toward designing premiere Web sites for its clients. As the bandwidth on the Internet continues to grow and ISDN, cable modems, and other high speed access becomes more prevalent, the demand for well-designed Web sites brimming with high quality and compelling content will skyrocket. The rich content currently delivered on CD-ROM and hard drives will be available to a broad Internet audience in as little as five years, as bandwidth increases.

Why Shockwave?

Shockwave offers the easiest and most cost-effective way to integrate sound, animations, simple and complex interactivity, and games and other activities into Web sites. 2-Lane Media has a staff highly proficient in all aspects of Macromedia Director and in producing small, floppy disk-sized presentations, so it makes economical and design sense to concentrate on taking the company's experience and talents with Director directly to the Web using

Shockwave. In order to reproduce Shockwave movies in Java, it would take at least twice the development time, involve more debugging and recoding, and cost a great deal more. Overall, it is much more effective, simpler, and easier, both in time and money, for multimedia production companies to add animations and interactivity to the Web using Shockwave rather than Java. While Java is great for complex database and interactivity, Shockwave will do most of the things Java can do, and do them faster, less expensively, and in some ways, better.

Shockwave Opportunities

Shockwave gives 2-Lane Media the opportunity to take the skills and the talents that our staff has honed over the past five years with Macromedia Director, producing CD-ROMs, IPKs, and other interactive productions and bring those talents and skills to the Internet. Shockwave will help 2-Lane Media to compete successfully in the industry of designing creative and top-quality World Wide Web sites by allowing us to keep our quality and creative standards high yet keep our costs manageable.

Shockwave enables our developers to add dynamic and creative interfaces with rollover highlights and animations to our clients' Web sites. In addition we can take our skill in producing small sized interactive games and activities and bring these to the World Wide Web. By adding interactive games and activities to our clients' Web sites, we can increase interest in the site, increase overall traffic to the site, and increase the time Web patrons stay at the site. In a sense, the flood gates are now open to many forms of interactive information, education, and entertainment content as a direct result of Shockwave. Net surfers need no longer be content with dull, static pages; they can now see motion, hear sound, and interact more than ever before.

Your Ideal Future on the Internet with Shockwave

The ideal future for Shockwave and the Internet would be a World Wide Web where all browsers seamlessly brought Shockwave to the Internet masses. In this way, all Web sites could be produced using Macromedia Director and Shockwave. Using special programmers to produce complex CGI and PERL scripts would be a thing of the past. Costs for producing complex sites with tracking mechanisms and search engines will drop using Shockwave. In a Shockwave world, companies with expertise in Macromedia Director can be among the most competitive and creative producers of Websites in the industry, and create exciting sites.

Project One: "Panic in the Park" for Warner*Active*

Warner*Active*: "Panic in the Park" Interactive Marketing Kit—Bust the Balloons Activity (Developed by William Patrick, Lisa Browning, David Lane)

Tips and Techniques from Real-World Shockwave Developers

Panic in the Park—Bust the Balloons Dart Game.

Movie Name: DART.DCR
Original File Size: 330K
Afterburned File Size: 127K
Percent File Compressed: 62%

Macromedia Shockwave for Director

"Panic in the Park" is a three-disc, interactive mystery CD-ROM title starring Erika Eleniak. It was developed by Imagination Pilots, and is published by Warner*Active*.

To promote this title, Warner*Active* enlisted the help of 2-Lane Media. 2-Lane Media opted to use Macromedia Director to create a floppy disk-sized interactive marketing kit. The marketing kit is now available for both the Macintosh and Windows platforms, and was designed for distribution on both floppy disks and on Warner*Active's* own Web site, http://www.warneractive.com/.

Within the first two months of its availability, the "Panic in the Park" interactive marketing kit was downloaded from Warner*Active's* Web site some 100,000+ times.

Recently, 2-Lane Media and its client, Warner*Active,* decided to take advantage of Macromedia's Shockwave technology. The companies chose an arcade activity from the "Panic in the Park" marketing kit, a dart-throwing game, and turned it into a Shockwave movie. The game itself resembles a traditional carnival arcade game where you throw darts at balloons and pop them, in this case to find a hidden special message.

This movie is now available on the World Wide Web, and dramatically displays the interactive power of Shockwave.

Project's goal

This interactive marketing kit was designed to promote Imagination Pilots' CD-ROM mystery game, "Panic in the Park." The kit had the additional task of advertising the Web site of "Panic in the Park's" publisher, Warner*Active*. Rather than merely demonstrating, this marketing piece was designed to give consumers the "flavor" of the 3D amusement park environments of the CD and the "feel" of its carnival arcade-style games and activities. The Marketing Kit proved an excellent way to make the "Panic in the Park" CD-ROM game stand out from its competitors.

Why did you use Shockwave for Director?

In order to place the "Bust the Balloons" onto the World Wide Web, the only clear choice for 2-Lane Media was to use Director and Shockwave.

Server push and client pull might handle simple animation readily enough, but this was more involved, and response times would have been exceedingly slow. Additionally, obtaining a qualified Java programmer would have been exceedingly expensive, and to replicate the game would have taken at least twice as long, and cost more.

Because the activity had already been produced in Director for the full "Panic in the Park" marketing kit, it was essentially seamless for us to turn the game into a Shockwave movie. All that was needed was to separate the activity from the rest of the marketing kit and narrow the stage dimensions so that the game would fit easily into a Web browser set for a 13" computer screen.

Tips and Techniques from Real-World Shockwave Developers

Software tools used

The entire "Bust the Balloons" and Marketing Kit was created using Macromedia Director. Supporting tools included Macromedia's Sound Edit 16 and Adobe's Photoshop.

Hardware used

No special hardware was required for production, other than a few Macintosh and Windows computers. Testing was performed on both the Macintosh and Windows machines.

Platforms

This piece was initially created on the Macintosh platform, with some development and other work performed on Windows. Testing occurred on both Macintosh and Windows machines, each running its native system software.

Technique: Creating a realistic dart game

"Panic in the Park" consists largely of arcade-style games and activities, similar to those seen in old-style amusement parks, as well as Myst-like, 3-D walkthroughs and interactions with characters in full screen, full motion video. The game is delivered on three CD-ROMs. 2-Lane Media faced the challenge of providing an arcade feeling to a floppy disk-sized interactive marketing kit.

Macromedia Shockwave for Director

The activity, which seemed to provide a straightforward approach to defining what is meant by "arcade," was the "Bust the Balloons" dart throwing game. Imagination Pilots developed some masterful games throughout "Panic in the Park." Their dart game was certainly no exception.

It was decided that the 2-Lane Media version of the dart game should match the original as closely as possible with Director. This was decidedly a challenge, especially because the original game is all custom C++ coded, and the dart game takes into account such factors as gravity, arcs, and aim. There are many such factors that need to be considered in a game of digital darts.

To accomplish this realism, there were several steps of an actual dart toss that needed to be replicated. For example, the player taking aim, the steadying of the throwing arm, the throw, the release, the dart's trajectory, and the dart hitting a target all needed to be duplicated.

In the "Panic in the Park" dart game, we had to determine the trajectory of the dart based on a number of different criteria, including how fast the game player threw the dart and if the player threw the dart straight or to the left or the right.

Step by step

1. Throughout the dart game, the player is able to move the throwing hand about, from left to right. This is how the player takes aim. The horizontal position of the cursor is stored, and the "player's hand" is moved about the screen to match.

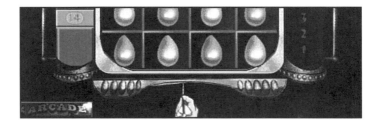

2. Before an actual dart toss, the thrower pulls back his or her hand to prepare the dart for flight. In the game, the action is no different. The player indicates readiness by pulling back on the mouse. The "hand" is pulled back, thus acknowledging the player's readiness.

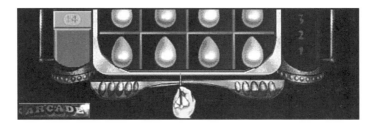

3. The player then pushes the mouse forward, mimicking a real-world dart release. With a timer and user interaction, the program determines how far the dart should travel. This procedure might be likened to a pressure-plate device from a favorite spy movie. After the player pulls back the mouse, the device is turned on—in this case, the dart is ready for a throw. When the player moves off the "plate" by pushing the mouse forward, a short countdown is begun. The player's vertical position is stored when the countdown is finished. This position determines the ultimate height and trajectory of the dart. A slowly moving mouse means you will have a low-flying dart. A quick release translates to a high-flying dart.

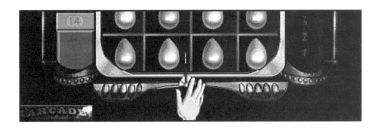

4. Showing the trajectory (and the ultimate destination) of the dart posed an interesting problem. The speed of the dart would be critical. Because a slowly moving dart could shatter the "arcade feel," it was important to give Director most of the player's computer processing timer. This section was therefore controlled solely by means of a script. This helped to prevent other running applications from "time sharing" the processor during frame updates. Ultimately, this lead to improved performance, even on the slower machines used in testing.

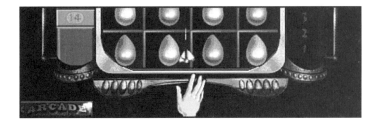

Project Two: The Fit Model for "The Spot" Web Site

The Fit Model: A Spot Shockwave Experience

(Developed by Scott Zakarin, Troy Bolotnick, Rik Shannon, and David Lane)

Movie Name: FITMODEL.DCR
Original File Size: 1219K
Afterburned File Size: 663K
Percent File Compressed: 46%

"The Spot" is one of the most popular Web sites on the Internet—Web Site URL: `http://www.thespot.com/`. Daily Variety describes "The Spot" as "an innovative episodic Netshow that has won a wide audience on the World Wide Web" (*Daily Variety,* June 12, 1995). The show is about a group of twenty-somethings who live in a Santa Monica beach house in California and chronicle their lives on the Internet through daily journal entries that include text, photos, sounds, and video. Among the Spotmates is sexy Michelle Foster who works as a fit model for a lingerie manufacturer. When the Spotmates decided to give their audience holiday gifts, they let the audience tell them what they wanted. In the case of Michelle, the overwhelming request was to see photos of her at work. Instead of just posting photos, Michelle, with the help of Spot Producers and 2-Lane Media, created The Fit Model. In The Fit Model, Spot fans can dress up Michelle in a variety of different lingerie and sleep wear. Set to a funky beat and loaded with hidden surprises, The Fit Model has been tremendously popular among The Spot audience.

Project's goal

The goal of The Fit Model was to entertain and engage Spotfans. The creators and producers of "The Spot," Scott Zakarin and Troy Bolotnick, chose to use Shockwave with the same philosophy they apply to all new Web technologies. "We don't just throw a new technology up there for the sake of technology. We find a way to use it in the story of 'The Spot' to make the experience entertaining and compelling—keep the audience coming back. Shockwave gives us a great opportunity to push the envelope and keep 'The Spot' on the cutting edge of the World Wide Web in both content and delivery."

Why did you use Shockwave for Director?

The type of activity contained in The Fit Model could not be produced cost-effectively by using Java. Director served as the fastest, simplest, and cheapest way to create a drag-and-drop game that included high quality graphics on the World Wide Web.

Software tools used

The entire Fit Model activity was created using Macromedia Director. Supporting tools included Macromedia's SoundEdit 16, Adobe's Photoshop and Debabelizer by Equilibrium.

Hardware used

No special hardware was required in the production.

Tips and Techniques from Real-World Shockwave Developers

Platforms

The entire Marketing Kit was developed on the Macintosh platform and then thoroughly tested on Windows.

Technique: Optimizing palettes for playback

In The Fit Model activity, we wanted to optimize the graphics for the best palettes possible. One Shockwave Director file contains two identical versions: one that runs under an 8-bit Windows System palette, and one that runs under an 8-bit custom palette. As of the release of this book, Web visitors viewing Shockwave files with their monitors set to 256 colors (8 bit) will see all the graphics in their Shockwave files dithered to either a Windows System palette or a Macintosh System palette, depending on which platform they are using. The custom palette will be seen only if the Web user views the Shockwave files in thousands of colors or more (16 bit or higher). The custom palette is preferable over a system palette, so we wanted to make this option available.

We decided not to create a third version using the Macintosh System palette because we felt that the Macintosh System palette was fairly close to the Windows System palette. We chose the Windows System palette over using the Macintosh System palette because there are just more Windows users than Macintosh users on the Internet, and we wanted to go with a palette that would look better for the greatest amount of people.

Using two sets of the same graphics for two different palettes makes your Shockwave file about twice as large. You should only take advantage of this method if there are graphics that you really want to look best in both 8 bit and 16 bit, and if the Windows System palette is not quite good enough.

Step by step

1. All of our original graphics had to start in either 16-bit or 24-bit color mode. From there we were able to create two sets of graphics, each using a different palette.
2. Using a program like Equilibrium's Debabelizer, we were able to create a custom palette based on all the original graphics. Using the custom palette, we were able to use Debabelizer to dither one complete set of graphics to the custom palette.
3. Using a program like Equilibrium's Debabelizer, we were able to dither one complete set of original graphics to the Windows System palette.
4. After importing the two sets of graphics into Director, we assembled the activity in the Score twice, the first time using the custom set of graphics and the second time using the Windows System palette. It is most effective if you lay out your activity once, duplicate it, and then use the *Switch Castmember* command to swap the cast members in the duplicated part of the Score.
5. If you are referring to palette colors by their number positions, you should verify that you are making the proper adjustments in your scripts for each of your sections. The palette numbers in a script may be fine for one palette but not another.

CL!CK Active Media

Goal:	To build an interactive educational Web site.
Developers' Names:	Claire Barry and Sven Krong
Company:	CL!CK Active Media
Address:	4605 25th Street Suite 1, San Francisco, CA 94114
Phone:	415-642-5947
Fax:	415-642-5948
Email:	claire@clickmedia.com, sven@clickmedia.com
Web Site URL:	www.clickmedia.com/

About CL!CK Active Media

Cl!CK Active Media is an interactive communications agency that is dedicated to providing advanced online experiences.

Company Focus

We bring multiple disciplines into sharp focus—Sven brings 10 years of film and television production and 8 years of multimedia programming. Claire brings 13 years of computer graphics experience and 5 years of marketing. Combined we have created award-winning projects in film, television, video, interactive CD-ROMs, kiosks, Internet Web sites, and more.

Clients and Projects

Our client list includes PCWorld, Virgin Interactive Entertainment, Pulse Entertainment, Sony Pictures Entertainment, 20th Century Fox Home Entertainment, Rocket Science, Gamespot, and NetGravity, among others.

Impact of the Internet

The Internet has had a huge impact on our company. The Internet has quickly become the largest percentage of our media services. Within the Internet business alone there is a huge field of services to develop and create.

Currently, the startling growth of the Internet has shifted many developers' focus from multimedia to the Internet. As the Shockwave Plug-In demonstrates, multimedia is ready today on the Internet, so thankfully all the lessons we have learned for optimizing content for CD-ROMs can apply to the Web and get everyone up to speed quickly.

Why Shockwave?

Shockwave for Director enables us to combine CD-ROM style interactivity with the incredible reach of the Internet. Because CL!CK has extensive CD-ROM design and authoring experience, it also leverages that knowledge base against the learning curve of Java. The best way of looking at the Shockwave vs. Java debate is to understand the strengths of each technology and understand what it takes to implement these technologies. To program a Java applet just to play a little animation with sound is a little heavy handed—Shockwave lets you do that with ease. But a multiplatform, self-contained promotional applet that allows users to order products, contains credit transaction capability, and provides detailed reporting would be a Java project for now.

Shockwave Opportunities

Shockwave enables us to make our sites more dynamic than anything else out there, therefore attracting the type of clientele we are interested in. It also helps us create these dynamic sites without the heavy programming efforts Java and VRML require. By conserving resources for the appropriate tasks, we can spend our precious time and energy on the most cost-effective solutions—and that's good for business growth.

Besides the initial impact of the shocked animated banners and site sound effects, Shockwave opens the door for more sophisticated interaction interfaces and information management. It also allows for persistent memory, which is something the rather stateless Internet could use. For example, within standard HTML/WWW pages there is no mechanism for doing rollover buttons or for tracking how long a user has been idle, etc. Incorporating a minuscule Shockwave movie in a Web page could give the page a brain—capable of extending the capabilities of the page transparently, acting in the background.

Your Ideal Future on the Internet with Shockwave

Persistent streaming, real-time, full-screen interactive Web pages. It seems to be a natural extension to take everything we've learned about communication, audio, graphics, text, video, and interactivity and mix that into a full bandwidth global interactive system, and *POW!* The virtual sky's the limit.

Project: Dream a Dolphin's New Media Internship Competition

Movie Name:	"Content.DCR"
Original File Size in Bytes:	111K
Afterburned File Size:	33K
Percent File Compressed:	69%

"Dream a Dolphin," which was founded by Toni Childs, invites a collaboration among universities, corporations, and foundations to support and empower children, therapists, and students at the university level in the use of new media technology. This Web site is an introduction and invitation to participate in the Internship Competition.

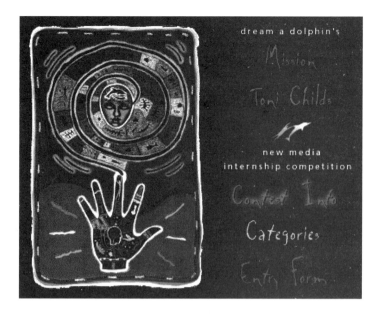

Project's goal

The goal was to repurpose the content from the CD-ROM we made for this project and convert it to the Web. Since the CD-ROM version was so compelling, we wanted to maintain the look and feel of the CD-ROM on the Net. Shockwave to the rescue.

Why did you use Shockwave for Director?

We used Shockwave because it represented a quantum shift in the look of the Web pages without a quantum leap in the cost to create them. Server pushes are best suited for animations, but each element that animates on a page requires an additional connection to the host server. Shockwave is much more efficient at that because after the shocked movie has been loaded there is no additional load on the server. Now the thought of using Java for a simple animation and a sound bite is ridiculous. Shockwave is just so much easier to use and implement—because the scrolling regions can't be implemented via server push, and using Java to do something Shockwave can do with ease is just inefficient.

Software tools used

We used Macromedia Director and Afterburner on the Mac to author and adapt the Shockwave movies, SoundEdit Pro to trim the audio and make the sound loops, Adobe Photoshop for the graphic element creation, Adobe PageMill for the site layout, and BBEdit to clean up the final Web pages.

Hardware used

The Director programming was done on a Quadra 900, the graphics were done on a PowerMac 7500, and the Shockwave testing was done on our Pentium PC.

Platforms

We used the Mac platform to develop and create all the programming and content, and used the PC platform to test the technology.

Technique: Custom scrolling text regions

Custom scrolling text regions are a sensible and impactful use of Shockwave in a Web page. They are functionally efficient because the text is contained within a limited region, therefore allowing other elements such as imagery and navigational elements to be continually present. It also adds visual interest to typically stale HTML-based pages.

Because all the principles for creating low-bandwidth GIF elements apply to creating Shockwave movies, the final file size is extremely compressed when Afterburned, in this example the entire Shockwave movie is only 33K. Low-bandwidth techniques include using flat system color, cropping elements tightly, and creating efficient Lingo scripts.

Step by step

1. The Border Base—Using a 24-bit image of the border, the exterior was pasted into a flat system palette color background, in this case blue. The interior was selected with an anti-aliased magic wand and filled with a light yellow from the system palette. The image was then converted to an 8-bit system PICT using diffusion dithering.

2. The Scroll Bar Elements—Four elements make up the scroll region: the vertical scroll bar, the up arrow, the down arrow, and a scroll handle object. The scroll bar and arrows are anti-aliased to the interior base color. The scroll handle object is aliased to white, and made transparent in Director using the Matte cast member option.

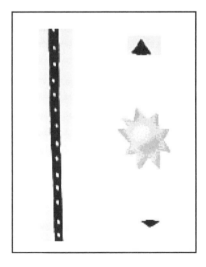

3. Director Element Integration—All the elements (the border base, the scroll elements, and the text) are brought together in Director. The various scrolling handlers are applied to the appropriate objects, and the Director file is saved.

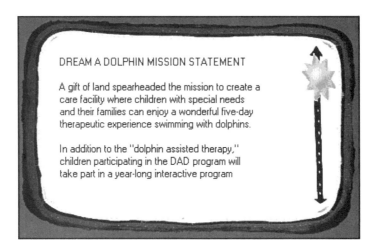

4. Integrating the movie into HTML—The movie is processed through Afterburner and integrated into the HTML page using the Embed command. Because the background color of the border base is a solid system color, it can be seamlessly placed into an HTML page with the same background color.

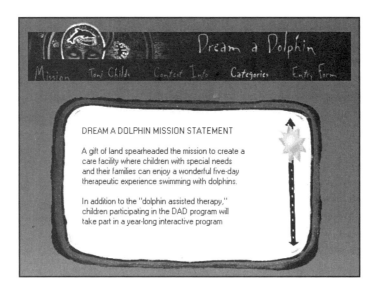

Fun facts

Longest Wait for a Download: 4 hours
Favorite Pastime while Downloading: Playing WipeOut! on the Playstation
Most Unusual Use for a Shockwave Movie: Still Image!
Web Site You Would Like to See "Shocked" the Most: Ours!

DAVIDEO

Goal: To generate complex "algorithmic animations" for high-impact visuals.
Developer's Name: David K. Anderson
Company: DAVIDEO
Address: 272 30th Street
Phone: 415-908-0492
Fax: 415-908-0495
Email: dkanderson@davideo.com
Web Site URL: http://www.davideo.com/

About DAVIDEO

DAVIDEO is a multimedia design and production company based in San Francisco.

Company Focus

We specialize in Macromedia Director-based interactive presentations, with an emphasis on high-quality Lingo scripting and 3D graphic design.

Clients and Projects

Most of our clients are in the media business. For Macromedia, we added interactivity to their Web site via Shockwave and scripted the Lingo for their award-winning Showcase CD-ROM. For other developers, such as The Judson Rosebush Company in New York, we've programmed the interactivity that made their productions for CBS, HBO, and others such a success. We also have created a series of screen savers that we market actively on the Net.

Impact of the Internet

The Internet has completely changed our business. We now conduct most of our transactions across the Net and have a worldwide network of clients, for whom we use the Internet to deliver our product. In addition, the Internet has proven to be an invaluable wellspring of information and other digital resources vital to our business. Our Web page is our most cost-effective means of advertising and connection to our clients. The Net is the heart of our business.

Why Shockwave?

Shockwave has enabled us to leverage our 10-year expertise in Macromedia Director and Lingo programming into an entirely new and growing market. And our experience in the creation of compelling, small-footprint content that will fit on a floppy disk (as we have done for CBS, Interactive Week, and others) segues very well with the bandwidth constraints that most users of the Internet are all too familiar with.

Shockwave Opportunities

In strictly technical terms, Shockwave takes advantage of the distributed nature of the Internet, with each user providing the processing power needed to run his own downloaded copy of a Shockwave presentation. With Java, the network is the computer, and users are at the mercy of the server to feed them the information they need. After a Shockwave movie is downloaded, that movie can be played as long as Netscape is running, even if the user goes "off-line." Additionally, Director is a mature authoring environment, time-tested, and reliable, so we are assured that our Shockwave movies will perform as designed.

Tips and Techniques from Real-World Shockwave Developers

Your Ideal Future on the Internet with Shockwave

I believe that Shockwave and other multimedia-based information is the future of the Internet. As bandwidth expands and as more users join the Internet, the opportunities for creators of content, such as those of us at DAVIDEO, is virtually limitless.

Project: Algorithmic Animations in Shockwave

Movie Name:	SPIRAL.DCR
Original File Size:	33K
Afterburned File Size:	8.5K
Percent File Compressed:	75%
Movie Name:	SAVER.DCR
Original File Size:	550K
Afterburned File Size:	264K
Percent File Compressed:	52%

At DAVIDEO, we specialize in "algorithmic animation," that is, animation driven by mathematical formulae via Lingo. This enables us to create Shockwave movies that have a very small size, but can display a startling variety of appearances and functionality.

Project's goal

An example of this "algorithmic animation" style of Shockwave movie is the pattern generator. The Shockwave movie draws an infinite variety of spiral patterns by using a Lissajou algorithm that uses only Lingo and the trace function in Director. For variety, we added five different drawing "pens" of different sizes and shapes. The entire movie compresses to 8.5K and can be downloaded even on the slowest dial-up in under five seconds.

We chose to use Shockwave for this project because of the ease of use of Director and Lingo. Creating a similar "applet" in Java would have required much more time and programming, if it could be created at all.

Software tools used

Most of the work on this project was done in Director; only one other program (Adobe Photoshop) was used to create the graphics.

Hardware used

We originally developed the movie on a 16 mHz Macintosh II several years ago. The scaleable nature of Director gives us the ability to play back this movie on almost any Macintosh or Windows machine from our old Mac II all the way up to a 150 mHz Windows box (where it performs much better, as you can imagine!).

Platforms

Windows and Macintosh.

Technique One: Randomizing patterns with Lingo

Here's the Lingo needed to make a bitmap move in a random spiral pattern around the screen.

Step by step

1. First, put this in the movie script:

1a. Global declarations.

```
global gTheta, gPhi, gR, gR2, gRep, gTempTheta, gTempPhi,
gPlayedOnce, gNumOTimes
```

1b. Set up globals and conditions.

```
on startmovie
  set the randomseed = the ticks
  set cStageWidth = the stageRight - the stageLeft
  set cStageHeight = the stageBottom - the stageTop
  set gPlayedOnce = 0
  set the floatPrecision = 7
  set gNumOTimes = 236
  set gRep = 0
  set gR = 150
  set gR2 = 150
  set gTempTheta = .001
  set gTempPhi = .25
end
```

1c. Prepare to draw.

```
on spiralInit
  puppetsprite 24, TRUE -- This is the "pen" sprite
  set the trails of sprite 24 to 1
  updateStage
  if gPlayedOnce = 1 then newValues
  -- Convert degrees to radians.
  set gTheta = gTempTheta * (pi()/180)
  set gPhi = gTempPhi * (pi()/180)
end
```

1d. The algorithm that controls the puppetsprite's location on stage:

```
on LissaJou2
  repeat with x = 1 to (gNumOTimes * pi())
    if the mouseDown then
      exit repeat
```

123

Macromedia Shockwave for Director

```
      else
        set gRep = gRep + 1
        set newH = gR2 * sin(100 * gTheta * gRep) * cos(100 * gPhi *
    ➥gRep) + ¬
    gR * sin(gTheta * gRep) * cos(gPhi * gRep) + 169 --(cStageWidth/2)
        set newV = gR2 * sin(100 * gTheta * gRep) * sin(100 * gPhi *
    ➥gRep) + ¬
    gR * sin(gTheta * gRep) * sin(gPhi * gRep) + 169 --(cStageHeight/2)
        set the loc of sprite 24 = point(newH, newV)
        updatestage
      end if
    end repeat
    set gPlayedOnce = 1
    set the loc of sprite 24 = point(-1000, -1000)
    go "Return"
  end
```

1e. Reset globals and choose a pattern and pen.

```
on newValues
  set whichPattern = random(24)
  if whichPattern > 4 AND whichPattern < 15 then set whichPattern = 5
  if whichPattern >= 15 then set whichPattern = 6
  set the castnum of sprite 24 = 129 + random(5)
  do "patternMaker" & whichpattern
end
```

1f. The values for the different patterns. The last two are random within a clamped limit.

```
on patternMaker1
  set gNumOTimes = 600
  set gRep = 0
  set gR = 150
  set gR2 = 20
  set gTempTheta = .3
  set gTempPhi = .5
end

on patternMaker2
  set gNumOTimes = 2300
  set gRep = 0
  set gR = 140
  set gR2 = 10
  set gTempTheta = .01
  set gTempPhi = 3
end

on patternMaker3
  set gNumOTimes = 572
  set gRep = 0
  set gR = 150
  set gR2 = 150
```

```
    set gTempTheta = .001
    set gTempPhi = 2
  end

  on patternMaker4
    set gNumOTimes = 2000
    set gRep = 0
    set gR = 150
    set gR2 = 40
    set gTempTheta = .01
    set gTempPhi = 1
  end

  on patternMaker5
    set gNumOTimes = 2000
    set gRep = 0
    set gR = 150
    set gR2 = random(30)
    set gTempTheta = log(random(100))/10
    set gTempPhi = log(random(100))
  end

  on patternMaker6
    set gNumOTimes = 2000
    set gRep = 0
    set gR = 150
    set gR2 = random(150)
    set gTempTheta = log((random(270)/100) + 1)/random(100) + .001
    set gTempPhi = random(100)/10
  end
```

2. Close the Movie Script window and add these scripts to the Score.
3. This script is placed in frame prior to the drawing frame:
   ```
   on exitframe
     spiralInit
   end
   ```
4. This is placed in the script of the frame where the drawing occurs:
   ```
   on exitframe
     Lissajou2
     go to the frame
   end
   ```
5. On the frame named "Return," I cover the screen with a black QuickDraw rectangle, which clears the trails. Also, I use a pixel dissolve in the Score to ease the transition. Then the playback head moves to the initialization frame.

Technique Two: Bouncing objects with Lingo

At DAVIDEO, we make a lot of screen savers with Director. Here's the Lingo needed to make a bitmap object appear to bounce off the edges of the screen.

Step by step

1. Put the following in the movie script of the Director file.

1a. First, set up the necessary global variables:

```
global gMySprite, gBound, gVelocityH , gVelocityV, gDirection
on startMovie
```

1b. Set the sprite number for the object.

```
set gMySprite = 24
puppetSprite gMySprite, TRUE
```

1c. Get the cast number of the bitmap that will move around the stage.

```
set baseCastNum = the number of cast ("My Object")
```

1d. Next, set the height and width of the object.

```
set baseWidth = (the width of cast baseCastNum)/2
set baseHeight = (the height of cast baseCastNum)/2
```

1e. Create a rectangle that is a subset to the stage.

```
set gBound = rect((the stageLeft + baseWidth),(the stageTop +
↪baseHeight), ¬
    (the stageRight - baseWidth), (the stageBottom - baseHeight))
```

1f. Finally, set the variables to impart an initial random velocity and direction for the object.

```
set gVelocityH = random(7)
set gVelocityV = random(7)
set randNum = random(2) - 1
if randNum then
 set gDirection = (-1)
else
 set gDirection = 1
end if
end

on animateObject
  set currentPositionH to the locH of sprite gMySprite + gVelocityH
  set currentPositionV to the locV of sprite gMySprite + gVelocityV

  if currentPositionH < getAt(gBound, 1) then
    set gVelocityH to -1 * gVelocityH
    set currentPositionH to getAt(gBound, 1)
  end if
```

```
if currentPositionV < getAt(gBound, 2) then
 set gVelocityV to -1 * gVelocityV
 set currentPositionV to getAt(gBound, 2)
end if

if currentPositionH > getAt(gBound, 3) then
 set gVelocityH to -1 * gVelocityH
 set currentPositionH to getAt(gBound, 3)
end if

if currentPositionV > getAt(gBound, 4) then
 set gVelocityV to -1 * gVelocityV
 set currentPositionV to getAt(gBound, 4)
end if

set the loc of sprite gMySprite to point(currentPositionH,
↪currentPositionV)

  updateStage

end
```

2. In the frame script for frame 1 in the Score, put the following script. (Be sure you have cast member "My Object" in channel 24 of frame 1 in the Score!)

   ```
   on exitFrame
    animateObject
    go to the frame
   end
   ```

3. If you've done everything correctly, the object should move about the stage and bounce off the sides!

Hands of Time

Goal:	To create cartoons of entertainment industry advertising
Developers' Names:	Janice Norton and Gary Ream
Company:	Hands of Time Animation & Design
Address:	3512 Sunset Blvd., Suite 133, Los Angeles, CA 90026
Phone:	213-483-2885
Fax:	213-483-1900
Email:	handsoftime@earthlink.net, HOT AD@aol.com
Web Site URL:	http://www.earthlink.net/~handsoftime/

Macromedia Shockwave for Director

About Hands of Time Animation & Design

Hands of Time Animation & Design (HOT AD) is a seven-year-old, privately owned multimedia company. Hands of Time pioneered interactive advertising for the entertainment industry with award-winning CD, floppy, Internet, and online-based promotions for motion pictures and television. Hands of Time designs for all markets, from traditional Fortune 500 clients, radio stations, and art museums to cutting edge MTV-style products geared toward the gen-X audience.

HOT AD has been awarded a slew of national new media awards for both design and programming in interactive advertising, including a Silver Cindy Award for technical excellence for fitting more on a floppy disk than had ever been done before, using Macromedia Director.

Company Focus

HOT AD's mission is to create exciting and challenging cross-platform (Mac and PC) multimedia products that are accessible for the average consumer. Though authoring for both platforms, we target and beta test our products first and foremost for the Windows market, and assume that the minimum playback machine will be a 486/66 with 8 MB of RAM and a double-speed CD-ROM player configured to display at 640×480 at 256 colors.

While the benchmark for multimedia is constantly changing, and we are immediately responsive to the newest technologies before they are introduced into the marketplace, we are sensitive to the technological limitations of the average user.

Just as Motown mixed their recordings to exploit the limitations of the average car radio, we create our multimedia pieces to excel on the average user's system. We push the envelope, creating small, efficient, well-designed files that will perform well on the typical playback platform—one that might have been under the Christmas tree a year earlier.

Clients and Projects

Hands of Time has created award-winning interactive promotions for the motion pictures of Martin Scorsese, Robert Altman, Mike Nichols, Rob Reiner, Jonathan Demme, Walt Disney, Stephen King, and the television shows of Brandon Tartikoff, Sam Raimi, and the BBC.

Hands of Time provided art direction and content for the MCA Television Internet site featuring the number one rated action/adventure hit *Hercules*. The site garnered an interactive academy award from the Academy of Interactive Arts & Sciences. Hands of Time highlights on the site included an extensive "virtual gallery" of original stereoscopic 3-D paintings, as well as a "Hercules in Babeland" area, a vast array of AVI and WAV files, and hundreds of megabytes of exciting, originally designed downloadables.

Recently, Hands of Time designed a spectacular 3-D Palace site for the Electronic Café, inviting the user into a hauntingly seductive world of ethereal beauty. The original paintings have the charm and innocence of a Maxfield Parrish fairy tale, intriguingly scattered with an array of fully functioning "techno-antiques" and other tempting interactive objects.

This site was used by the Electronic Café for an event linking more than eight countries worldwide to play in interactive, three-dimensional space. Hands of Time principals Janice Norton and Gary Ream teamed up with Palace programmer Tod Foley in the creation of this virtual meeting space, and are now offering professional Palace site development. The three are becoming rapidly known internationally by Palace users as "The Multimedia Mod Squad."

Hands of Time Animation & Design offers official Macromedia Shockwave development, multimedia animation and programming, interactive project management, art direction/Web site design, interface design, and radio advertising.

Professional Recognition

National Awards—Interactive Design and Programming

- Ad Age Magazine's Interactive Advertising & Media Award
- Academy of Interactive Arts & Sciences Award nomination—floppy disk
- Academy of Interactive Arts & Sciences Award finalist—Web site
- New Media Magazine's Invision Award
- Silver CINDY Award—floppy disk
- CINDY Award—CD

National ADDY Award

- First Place—Public Service Category
- Producer, art director, and original concept creator for "Baby Bottle" commercial

American Advertising Federation National Convention

- First Place—G.D. Crain, Jr. Public Service Advertising Award
- Second Place—Advertising Newsletter Production

ARC of the U.S.

- Outstanding Public Service Award

American Federation of Television and Radio Artists American Scene Award

Impact of the Internet

The Internet is a totally amazing tool for global communication. It liberates us to think and live on entirely different levels. As designers, we can put our portfolios online, we can share our vision with others, and interact in a shared space without leaving our homes...the Net takes us into a world reminiscent of my favorite Ray Bradbury stories!

Why Shockwave?

Shockwave is the next step in multimedia authoring for the Internet. Shockwave is inherently superior in the quality and range of animation it can offer. However, HOT AD will use many technologies on the Net, depending upon what is most appropriate to the project at hand.

Shockwave offers an infinite number of possibilities for creating exciting content on the Net, and as new applets become available or it becomes necessary to create them, we will do it. HOT AD will use whatever product is best able to achieve the effect we want to create.

Shockwave Opportunities

First of all, we would like to praise Macromedia for bringing real animation to the Web and creating an easy to install, free plug-in for the end user to enjoy. As developers, this is of utmost importance to us because we want to provide an enjoyable experience for the average user.

Most people are a little intimidated by the Net and by computers in general. The Shockwave Plug-In is easy to use; consequently, computer users in general and especially PC users, can install and use Shockwave without fear that they will have to reconfigure their system the next time they want to type a letter or play a game like "Doom" on their computer.

As online-based developers, we have faced a problem when using Director: The player (the stand-alone application added to the Director movie to make it playable without any other software) adds 600K to the movie size for Windows users. More troubling still, the player will only compress about one percent—a 6K savings. In earlier versions of the PC software, the player only added about 300K and compressed nicely.

For cross-platform developers, this has been doubly problematic because the Mac player still adds only about 300K and compresses nicely. Consequently, when restricted by disk space or bandwidth, the developer is left with two choices: tell the client that the PC version will be inferior to the Mac version, or strip down the Mac version to mirror the inferior PC version.

Shockwave has solved this problem for online development by first eliminating the player element from the file altogether, and by the creation of the Afterburner compressor, which gives a compression ratio nearly as good as PKZIP or StuffIt, yet doesn't require the movie to be uncompressed to play.

Your Ideal Future on the Internet with Shockwave

The possibilities seem endless. For example, Hearst Communications are supportive of cable modems—with increased speeds almost anything seems possible. Shockwave is still early in its development, but as time goes by, even with current networking technologies, we hope that later versions will do things like stream live over the Net (like director view did), incorporate Midi, enable the playback of externally linked files like QuickTime Musical Instruments and QuickTime, or better yet, MPEG. Also, we want support for Accelerator files again, as well as support for custom palettes and to build off the real audio sound compression technology.

Macromedia Shockwave for Director

Project: Satan's 666 Pack Animations

Movie Name:	"Slots of Sin"
Original File Size:	545K
Afterburned File Size:	245K
Percent File Compressed:	about 60%

Tips and Techniques from Real-World Shockwave Developers

Movie Name: "Fishbowl"
Original File Size: 2.7 MB
Afterburned File Size: 1.2 MB
Percent File Compressed: about 44%

Project's goal

Both the "Slots of Sin" and "Fishbowl" are parodies of industry advertising. Originally planning for a Halloween Shockwave roll-out, we created "Satan's 666 Pack," which is a whimsical demonstration of six different games and activities, such as painting, concentration, a crossword puzzle, etc. The project is only about 666K, our target number, and the file was designed with streaming in mind. Consequently, in the next version of Shockwave with streaming capabilities, the user would experience no wait-time. The project also featured a soundtrack with an intentionally "out of whack," tinny sound, designed to complement the candy wrapper style graphics.

"Slots of Sin" was originally conceived of as an URL randomizer using client pull to continually change a number of hot links to sites, thus offering examples of sites related to each of the seven deadly sins. Using Shockwave's navigation and animation capabilities, we expanded this idea into a full-fledged slot machine that enables the user to gamble to acquire tokens leading to increasingly tantalizing and amusing URLs, beginning with sloth and ending with lust.

Macromedia Shockwave for Director

Why did you use Shockwave for Director?

We used Shockwave rather then push-pull, and so on, because it is inherently superior in the quality and range of animation it can offer. We have avoided server push largely because of the time and expense of creating PERL scripts and the reluctance of most service providers to allow the execution of those scripts by their server. Moreover, the animation achieved by server push is not that exciting, and while it is useful for things like the "fish cam," for our purposes it was more trouble than it was worth.

We experimented with client pull, which eliminated the necessity of dealing with the network administrator, but it was also far more limited in what it would allow us to do.

Shockwave is easier and better. Moreover, Shockwave eliminates the necessity for the end user to acquire any particular helper application for sound, etc. It's plug and play. We believe that this is extremely important because most users of the Net and of computers want something that is simple. For new users especially, simplicity is key.

Software tools used

We used Adobe Photoshop, SoundEdit Pro, and Macromedia Director.

Hardware and platforms used

We authored on a Quadra 700 and cross-checked all files on a IIci. We chose these older, lower-end platforms to keep what is happening during the production process from getting too far afield from what the project will eventually have to be (that is, it may work on your new, expensive graphic station, but most people's computers are typewriters with game playing and networking capabilities, not graphics stations). We then beta tested it on a number of platforms, including several PowerMacs and a 486/66 and a 386, and were happy with the results.

Technique: Small sounds for even smaller files

Shockwave is not really that different from a typical multimedia kit that would have to fit on a floppy disk or that would be downloaded off the Net. There are, however, limitations that make Shockwave a little more challenging. Perhaps the most daunting of these challenges is the issue of small sound files.

Originally, the "Slots of Sin" project also featured a MIDI soundtrack with an intentionally "out of whack," tinny sound, designed to complement the candy wrapper style graphics. While MIDI sounds tinny at best, we took advantage of this tinny sound by modeling the use of MIDI after that of "DEVO" or "The Residents," thus making the style and technology reinforce content, in much the same way as the German expressionists.

As Shockwave release time neared, it became increasingly clear that "Slots of Sin" wasn't going to work with the beta version of Shockwave because the initial version of Shockwave did not support MIDI or externally linked QuickTime Musical Instruments movies. However, this is planned for the next version of Shockwave in mid-1996.

Because we couldn't use MIDI in "Slots of Sin," we decided to go for a bongo drum WAV file, which, though short, would enable us to create a random "Beatnik" type of sound as it looped and added a substantial number of other short provocative sounds that could be repeated to create an expressive overall effect. This also helped us save on the Afterburned file size because sound files do not compress very well.

Step by step

For doing a project that requires small, yet impactful sound files:

1. Edit your original sound down to form a new "loop" or a short sound effect. This can be done in any sound editing program.
2. After you have completed your new sound loop or effect, dither the sound down to 8 bits, 11kHz to make it as small as possible.
3. Import your new AIF or WAV file into Director and then place it as needed in your movie. Before you save the file be sure to clean out any unused sounds to help decrease the final file size.

M/B Interactive

Goal:	To create an immersive musical experience for Sony Music
Developer's Name:	François Balmelle
Company:	M/B Interactive
Address:	122 East 25th Street, New York, NY 10016
Phone:	212-253-0200
Fax:	212-253-0941
Email:	balmelle@mbinter.com
Web Site URL:	http://mbinter.com/

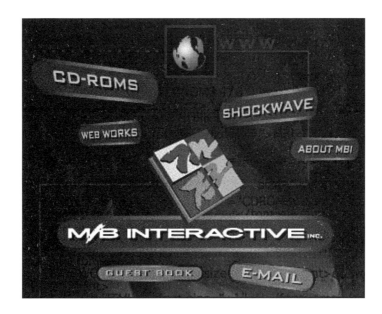

About M/B Interactive

M/B Interactive is a collection of professionals from converging fields. Under one roof, we combine concept, graphics, programming, marketing, and advertising. Our products are high-quality content that suits today's culture and creates tomorrow's.

Company Focus

M/BI's primary focus is creative content development—because no matter how much the technology changes, the one thing that remains constant is the importance of a strong creative concept. Our multimedia specialties include CD-ROM/enhanced CD production, and Internet Web site development.

Clients and Projects

Sony Music/Deep Forest Web Site

FreeRide Media/FreeRide Web Site

Creative Media/Creative Media Web Site

Spring Street Brewing Co./Wit Beer Web Site

Philips Media, Island Records/the Cranberries "Doors and Windows" enhanced CD

Deutche Grammaphon/Orpheus "Vivaldi's Winter Movement" CD-ROM

TG Media/ "The Ledgerbook of Thomas Blue Eagle" CD-ROM

Impact of the Internet

With increasingly more sophisticated tools and access to greater bandwidth, the Internet's ability to deliver real-time multimedia is growing fast. Soon CD-ROM content and performance will be available online. As a result, our company is shifting its emphasis away from CD-ROM production to online production.

The Internet has begun to evolve out of a "print" metaphor into a "broadcast" metaphor. Companies that are in the business of creating Web "pages" are going to have to learn how to create Web "channels." This is a whole different way of thinking and communicating. The players in this game are definitely going to change.

Why Shockwave?

To begin, we already had years of experience working with Director. It's a tool that's been around for a long time. There's also a lot of other people out there who already know how to use Director. This makes it easy for us to draw upon this large pool of designers and programmers who can immediately help us out if we need it. But what's most important is Director's capability to work as a high-level design tool. Unlike many other authoring tools, you don't have to be a programmer to create content in Director. Its highly intuitive environment enables our creative team to concentrate on the design and concept, rather than being bogged down with complicated code-writing.

Shockwave Opportunities

Any clients who want to make a real impact on the Internet are going to have to "shock" their Web sites. After people can view images on their Web browsers, do you think they will want to spend time at text-only sites? The same will be true with Shockwave. Users are going to be attracted to Web sites that can give them this new level of experience and interaction.

Shockwave is giving the Web a whole new look and feel. Currently, you have motion, sound, and more sophisticated interactivity than just hypertext links. From a designer's standpoint this opens the door to doing some really fun stuff. Finally, the Web is truly going to be transformed into a multimedia environment. This will attract more users, more marketers, and more money.

Your Ideal Future on the Internet with Shockwave

Ideally, M/BI will have a complete monopoly on creating content on the Web with Shockwave and will grow into the largest business empire in the known galaxy. ;-) How will that happen? Shockwave will turn a computer screen and the Internet into what people now think of as Interactive TV.

Project: Deep Forest Web Site for SONY Interactive

Name	Original Size	Afterburned Size	Percent Compressed
DFHUB.DIR	314K	165K	47.5%
DFNAV.DIR	50K	17K	66%
DFCD1.DIR	248K	149K	40%
DFCD2.DIR	330K	215K	35%
DFBIO.DIR	297K	198K	34%
DFSTUDIO.DIR	314K	182K	42%
DFMIXER.DIR	479K	297K	38%
DFTOUR.DIR	281K	165K	41.3%
PIGLAW.DIR	429K	248K	42.2%

Macromedia Shockwave for Director

We created a site for the French band "Deep Forest." Their ground-breaking albums combine modern dance music with ethnic sounds from around the globe, including Zaire, the Central African Republic, Hungary, Byelorussia, Taiwan, Japan, Bali, Georgia, and Mongolia. The purpose of the site was to deliver information about the band, including tour dates, interviews, discography, music samples, and information on a special interest of theirs, African pygmies.

Project's goal

We wanted to give people a much more immersive experience than what you get with a typical band's home page. Obviously, it's much more interesting to listen to a band than to read about it. Shockwave allowed us to add motion and sound, which was necessary to get a true feel for "Deep Forest" and what they're about. With Shockwave, we were also able to include a special sound mixer so that people could truly experience interactive music. Given the band's worldwide appeal, part of the challenge was to make the site accessible to an international audience. So we made extensive use of graphic symbols and icons. This, combined with Shockwave's sound and animation capabilities, helped us to better communicate across multilingual lines.

Why did you use Shockwave for Director?

We only had a week to do the project. Director puts control of the content directly in the designer's hands.

Software tools used

Macromedia Director, Macromedia SoundEdit, Macromedia Afterburner, Adobe Photoshop, Adobe Illustrator, HTML Editor

Hardware used

Power Macintosh 8100/80AV Pentium 100 PC

Platforms

Mac and PC.

Technique: Animating and colorizing one-bit cast members

Animating and colorizing one-bit cast members from a scan of a black-and-white image faxed from the illustrator, Frederic Voisin, in the U.K.

Step by step

1. Import image into the Director Cast. Make sure that the image's Color Depth is 1-bit. You can set this under the Transform Bitmap command under the cast menu.

2. Place cast member onto the Stage.

3. With the cast member still selected, you can colorize it using the Palette tool.

4. By varying the position and changing the color across time in the Score, you can create a very nice animation effect out of a simple black-and-white image.

Fun facts

Longest Wait for a Download: 1 hour, and that's only because I was using a 28.8 modem.

Favorite Pastime while Downloading: Listening to a good acid-jazz tune.

Most Unusual Use for a Shockwave Movie: There is not such a thing.

Web Site You Would Like to See "Shocked" the Most: I want to shock the White House.

NewOrder Media

Goal:	To create an interactive corporate advertisement
Developers' Names:	Kelly Michael Stewart, Phil Makes
Company:	NewOrder Media
Address:	209 Tenth Avenue South, Suite 450
	Nashville, Tennessee 37203
Phone:	615-248-4848
Fax:	615-248-6833
Email:	neworder@neworder.com
Web Site URL:	http://www.neworder.com/~neworder/

About NewOrder Media

NewOrder Media is an award-winning multimedia developer specializing in interactive solutions design.

Company Focus

NewOrder has achieved distinction as a premier interactive solutions firm by developing unique multimedia systems for clients as diverse as health care companies, law firms, and manufacturing concerns. By applying cutting-edge knowledge of interactive technologies, NewOrder has created information-rich kiosks, powerful networked training systems, and impact-oriented presentation systems. New information delivery techniques and platforms are emerging at a pace beyond initial predictions. To meet these challenges, NewOrder Media has assembled a talented team of specialists, including software designers, artists, hardware integrators, programmers, scriptwriters, technology consultants, and interactive designers. Our goal is to provide our clients with the competitive advantage through more efficient communication methodology.

Clients and Projects

Our clients include Mosby-Yearbook, Vanderbilt University, REN Corporation, Ethicon Endo-Surgery of Johnson & Johnson, HCA Center for Research and Education, Honeywell, Chrysler Technologies Airborne Systems, MagneTek, Medical Information Management Systems, Inc., Fluor Daniel, Deloitte & Touche, Centennial Medical Center, and Willis Corroon.

Our wide variety of project experience includes multimedia presentations, interactive learning solutions, kiosks, CD-ROM– and floppy–based marketing products, Web sites, and screen savers.

Impact of the Internet

We see the Internet as yet another delivery vehicle. In the past it provided an audience with up-to-the-minute information, although usually in text and simple graphic form. Therefore, being an interactive multimedia company, the Internet served as little more than a research and marketing tool. However, with the advent of Shockwave and the advancement of Internet technology, the World Wide Web is quickly becoming a viable and cost-effective delivery vehicle for our interactive multimedia services.

As public awareness, technology, and adoption of the Internet expand, we foresee our use of traditional media such as the CD-ROM diminishing, replaced by the more accessible and adaptable Internet. The multimedia business has thrived on interactivity. However, this has been limited by the confines of storage space and read-only media, which led to users being bound to the control of the developer. While the Internet as a delivery vehicle offers a virtually unlimited environment for developers, more importantly, users are able to control the boundaries of their communication in regards to the content with which they interact. This is crucial in our business as we attempt to meet the increasing demands of our clients. For example, our learning solutions are presently limited to dedicated training sites equipped with necessary software and the latest multimedia hardware. The future of the Internet will eliminate the complexity, allowing a more true "on-demand" and self-seeking system. For example, as employees are completing company-required training, they can go outside the prescribed lessons to locate related information elsewhere.

Why Shockwave?

We have over five years' experience using Macromedia Director, so it was a natural progression for us to go with a known quantity. Also, you don't have to be a programmer to use Director. Creative people are able to quickly develop engaging content using the program. Furthermore, we have been very pleased to see Macromedia continue to expand its software suite to embrace new technology such as Internet delivery.

Shockwave movies not only enable animated graphics and improved user feedback with rollovers and the like, but also we are able to do intelligent calculations with Lingo that don't require response from the server. Shockwave movies also are smaller and quicker compared to emulating the same visual appearance using GIFs and image maps.

Shockwave Opportunities

It is an obvious business decision for a multimedia developer to begin delivering content via the World Wide Web. Customers have begun to turn the hype of the Internet into real projects, and the cost of entry for us and for our clients was not insurmountable. Furthermore, with the advent of Shockwave, we are able to utilize our current knowledge of Director to create real multimedia material for Internet delivery. Our company will grow based on the fact that we can offer yet another viable delivery vehicle for multimedia.

Shockwave adds a new dimension to every one of our potential projects. Instead of simply creating a CD-ROM–based marketing piece, for instance, we can now say to our clients, "How about a multimedia Web site with the same look and feel of your CD, that also provides weekly updates to your customers?!"

We also see a huge opportunity for us in developing interactive learning products for corporations. Not only can we create new multimedia training content that can be delivered on the Net, but we can also repurpose our previous titles and deliver that content to a wider audience.

Your Ideal Future on the Internet with Shockwave

As the delivery pipeline gets bigger, compression technologies get better, and customer acceptance becomes broader, we foresee a day when we don't have to create different versions of our content based on limitations of the delivery medium. Therefore, the ideal future would be that Internet throughput could be identical or greater than we currently have from CD-ROM.

Project: Shockwave, the Motion Picture for NewOrder Media

Movie Name:	"NOMShock.dir"
Original File Size:	185K
Afterburned File Size:	99K
Percent File Compressed:	46%

Project's goal

This was an initial project to test the capabilities of Shockwave to market ourselves on our Web site.

Why did you use Shockwave for Director?

We are very familiar with Director and trust the Macromedia family, so it was an obvious choice for us. We also wanted more visual appeal with animated button feedback, spinning logos, and the unlimited capabilities that Lingo could allow.

Software tools used

Director, Photoshop, Debabelizer, SoundEdit, Extreme 3D, and FreeHand.

Hardware and platforms

We develop concurrently on Macintosh and Windows PCs.

Technique: Copy text to clipboard in Shockwave

We used the Lingo command copyToClipboard to allow users to click on one button and copy our contact information to their local clipboard.

Step by step

1. Type or paste the text you want the end user to copy into a text cast member.

2. Name the text cast member something obvious, such as "MyInfoText."

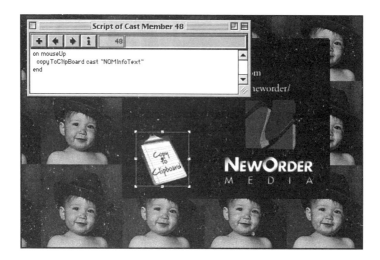

3. In the cast script of your Copy to clipboard button, use the following syntax:
    ```
    on mouseUp
      copyToClipBoard cast "MyInfoText"
    end
    ```
    where "MyInfoText" is the name of the text cast member containing the contact info.

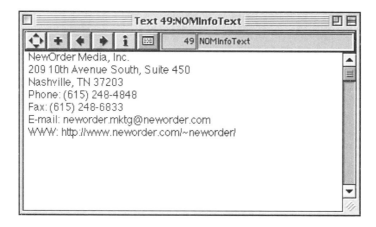

This is especially valuable when you want text cast members in your Director movie to hold more detailed information than you can display or even for an "on-the-fly" container for calculations, data collected, or variables.

Saturday!

Goal:	To reinvent classic arcade games like Tetris and Asteroids
Developer's Name:	Dan L. Berlyoung
Company:	Saturday!
Address:	965 Hunt Street, Akron, Ohio, 44306
Phone:	216-785-1326
Fax:	216-785-7282
Email:	1dan@mailhost.net
Web Site URL:	http://www.mailhost.net/~1dan/

About Saturday!

Saturday! is my part-time consulting business that keeps me current with the latest technology and visible in the local business community. I started out doing technical support for a local computer retailer and then for a vertical market integrator. Gradually, I moved over into the multimedia end of things, working with MPEG, Authorware, laserdiscs, and CD-ROM writers along the way. I spent the last year working on an educational children's game that was entirely done in Director. And living in Director for 12 months teaches you a thing or two. So I decided to go back to college and get my Masters and consult on the side. I am in the process of earning my Masters in Instructional Technology at Kent State University.

Company Focus

I've always enjoyed staying on the leading edge of computer technology, so renting myself out as a "technology connoisseur" was a logical thing. Director, Shockwave, Java, and the "Net," in general, are the hot things. But five years (maybe fewer) from now they won't be, and something else will be hot. So, I ride the wave and try to keep in front of everybody else and help them get to where I am.

Clients and Projects

Saturday!'s clientele ranges from rock and roll bands to major corporations—really, anyone who wants to get a message out to the world. Some want to squeeze it onto a single floppy disk, others want to use a whole CD. And now they have the Net, which along with an incredible list of advantages has an equally large set of limitations.

Impact of the Internet

Working with Director and creating multimedia titles was my primary focus until the Internet and the Web hit and changed everything. Shockwave has opened up an entirely new direction for me to go. The Internet is not so much a new tool, but a new kind of paper and printing press. I feel like one of the original printers with his brand-new Gutenberg press. The possibilities are (big surprise) endless.

Why Shockwave?

Shockwave and Java are two complementary products. The trick is to be familiar enough with both to make an intelligent decision on which to use for any particular project.

Shockwave Opportunities

Shockwave was a logical expansion of Director. The Web is graphic by nature, and Director was a logical tool to use. It just needed a few crucial enhancements to make it a Net tool. The incredibly small number of commands that had to be added to Lingo is an excellent example of how close the fit was.

Your Ideal Future on the Internet with Shockwave

Java, while powerful and flexible, will require a large investment of my time to master. Shockwave, on the other hand, has required little or no real investment of time to become proficient in, considering I already knew Director well.

Tips and Techniques from Real-World Shockwave Developers

Project: Arcade Games in Shockwave

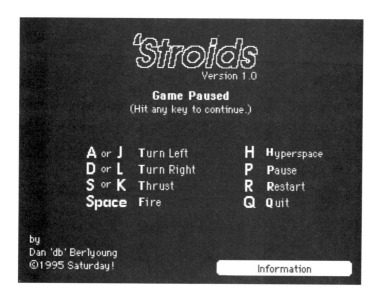

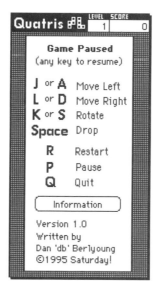

Movie Name:	"'Stroids"
Original File Size:	171K
Afterburned File Size:	71K
Percent File Compressed:	39%

Movie Name:	"Quatris"
Original File Size:	77K
Afterburned File Size:	27K
Percent File Compressed:	65%

Project's goal

The two games I created, "Quatris" and "'Stroids," were the result of a good guess and a surprisingly few number of hours. "Quatris" started out as a game I wrote in BASIC on an Apple II some eight years ago. I figured rewriting it would be a good exercise. It turned out to be a bit more challenging than I had initially thought, but nevertheless, I finished it. And I was more than a little surprised with its final size and playability.

Heartened by this first success, I then went on to write "'Stroids"—a re-creation of the venerable arcade game from yesteryear. This game presented a new set of challenging but not insurmountable problems—my main fear was the speed factor, but with the presence of several comments from users out on the Web asking me to "slow it down," this seems not to be a problem.

Why did you use Shockwave for Director?

I had heard several rumors that Macromedia was going to bring Director to the Web somehow. And judging from the bandwidth available now I figured that the movies would have to be as small as possible. So, I decided to see how far and how small I could take Director.

Software tools used

BASIC, Director, Afterburner.

Hardware used

Apple II.

Platforms

Macintosh.

Technique One: Maximizing channel usage in "Quatris"

The main hurdle I had to overcome while writing "Quatris" was the simple fact that the "Quatris" playing field consisted of a 10 by 20 grid containing 200 individual blocks that had to be completely independent of each other.

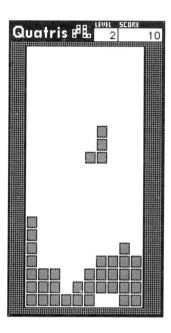

Accomplishing this was simple for a bit-mapped screen, but Director has, as we are all painfully aware of, only 48 sprite channels. I ended up being able to do it with only 40 tracks with 8 leftover for interface elements.

The inspiration for the solution came from the high-resolution graphics screen of the Apple II. It represented each pixel of the screen with a bit from a byte of memory. That way one byte could handle 7 pixels. (One pixel was for a color-shifting mechanism that is too arcane for me to go into now.) Remembering this I thought, "Why can't I do this with a sprite channel in Director?"

And that's what I did.

To start, I created 32 sprites that contained cast members, which represented all the ways that 5 blocks (or pixels) could be turned on and off.

Macromedia Shockwave for Director

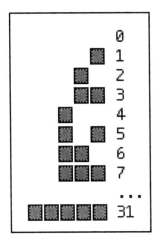

For example, the first actor had nothing in it, no blocks turned on. [ ] The second, had the first block turned on [x], the third [x], the fourth [xx], and so on up to the 32nd [xxxxx].

Then all I needed was to code up several binary Boolean functions so I could turn on and off specified bits inside the number that would represent which cast member I would use. (Namely, I needed a binary AND function to turn on and off specified bits.) By using this method I could handle 10 blocks (one of 20 rows) with only two sprite channels. At two channels per row and 20 rows, this comes out to 40 channels.

After creating those basic routines, the rest of the game was a simple matter of creating a main event loop that checked the keyboard, updated any falling shapes, and checked for collisions and completed rows.

Technique Two: Parent/child objects in "'Stroids"

The main challenge to writing "'Stroids" was that I had to be able to manage a variable number of objects all with different locations, appearances, velocities, and life spans. The key word here was "objects" and that meant using the dreaded "Parent/child" object-oriented part of Lingo that we all love and fear.

What I developed was an object called an "Oid" that represented a visible, moving thing on the screen.

This object, when "birthed" first searched for an open sprite channel and grabbed it. It then set up some location, velocity, and appearance properties, depending upon values sent to it. I could have had it insert itself into the "actor list" list, but I wanted to keep the "rocks" and "bullets" separate, so I maintained two lists that contained references to each object in these two classes.

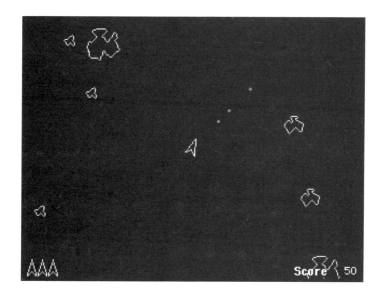

As with "Quatris," the game consisted of a main event loop that looked for key presses and sent update messages to all objects on the screen. The objects themselves took care of movement, collision checking, and lifetime expirations (bullets). The thing that shocked me the most while writing this game was that the bulk of the "Oid" object definition and the main event loop took only four hours to write. The remaining 10 hours or so were spent adding all the fluff—like scoring, number of ships remaining, and figuring out how to split one asteroid into two more while moving at slightly different vectors.

Using this same dynamic sprite allocation object definition (Oid) I am working on a "Missile Command" type game and am finding it also equally easy to create.

Fun facts

Longest Wait for a Download:	2 hours
Favorite Pastime while Downloading:	Reading the *Hacker's Dictionary*
Most Unusual Use for a Shockwave Movie:	Playing "'Stroids" on my Web page
Web Site You Would Like to See "Shocked" the Most:	The Dilbert Page (Just imagine 3D rotating Dogberts!)

Chapter 10

The Next Wave—Shockwave 2.0

With the extremely rapid expansion of the Internet and multimedia, the future possibilities for Shockwave are only limited by your imagination. Or, rather, the imagination of Macromedia Shockwave developers. Open your mind for a moment and look back at the Internet one year ago. "The Internet?" A year ago this word wasn't even known. Now, today, it seems as if the Internet is everywhere. At schools, on TV commercials and on billboard advertisements. And if you haven't figured out the Net yet, ask your kids for some help. They will probably know how to access the Net, as well as have their own email addresses. The popularity of the Internet is due in part to the fact that it's not controlled by any one corporation or individual. The Internet is a synergy of all its contributors, which makes it a place for pure, unbiased communication and information exchange. Everyone is equal on the Net, and everyone can have an opinion regardless of age, sex, religion, etc. This may sound scary, but you only need to be frightened by the Net for two reasons. One, if you don't know how to access it, and two, if you have something to hide. There are no secrets on the Net.

Future Possibilities for Shockwave and the Internet

The possibilities on the Net are endless. Here's where we think the Net is heading. The Internet has attracted the attention of every major corporation in the world. They all know that if they aren't on the Net now, that some day soon they will be. Add this to the development of Shockwave and cable modems, and you have interactive movies and information hitting every TV in the world. If you increase the speed of the cable modem, the home page of today automatically becomes the TV channels of tomorrow. With future versions of

Shockwave being pumped through cable modems, users will be able to visit your home page (through their television), read any information that is there, watch any videos, play any games, chat with the world, and maybe even order some pizza. If everyone is gravitating toward the fast, convenient, and relatively free method of being (or advertising) on the Net by having a home page, then the Net is gravitating toward becoming the TV of the 21st century. It's not hard to see the opportunity that the Net will offer. And at the rate the Net is growing and becoming popular, this will happen easily before the year 2000.

Shockwave may only offer small movies today, but this is not a Shockwave limitation—the limitation occurs because the speed limit of the information superhighway today is too small. Future Shockwave development plans could include the following features (in order of importance):

- **Compression for audio**—Audio compression will reduce the size of your movies even more.
- **XObject support**—Including real audio, video streaming, and QuickTime. Real audio will allow the streaming and playback of audio in real time. Video streaming will allow real-time playback of video.
- **Frame window control**—This feature will allow you to control the new framing window feature in Netscape 2.0.
- **Adding Shockwave's Lingo to Director**—This will allow you to program your Shockwave movie in Director and not get compiling errors.
- **Internationalization**—Support for Japanese, French, etc.
- **Windows NT**—16-bit support.

By the time Macromedia adds these features, the cable modem will be ready for the public, and you can be far ahead of the competition.

The Insider's Profile: The Shockwave Scoop

Who really invented "Shockwave?"

Bruce Hunt: Harry R. Chesley

Harry Chesley: Shockwave isn't an invention in and of itself. It's a bridge between Director and the Internet—two large bodies by functionality, concepts, and people. Bringing the two together expands the possibilities exponentially.

John Newlin: Good question. What do you mean invented? Christian Hunt and David Walker had a Director movie player out on the Web over a year ago. Does that count? Lalit suggested embedding Director into Netscape a long time ago, and Harry was hired to do something neat with the Internet, but his first thing to do was the Director Internet Player, which was going to be a stand-alone helper application. I, on the other hand, created the first Netscape plug-in, which is the basis for what Shockwave has evolved into. So I did the first implementation....

Sherri Sheridan: Harry—from realizing the value of the Web and Director's ability to play a part in this future.

Ken Day: As far as the basic feature set and concepts of Shockwave, Harry pretty much laid that out. The internal design of the new components—Harry, Sarah, and I together designed how the bits would flow.

When was it originally invented?

BH: Fall of '94.

HC: The project started in early '95.

JN: What do you mean by invented? If you mean the first Netscape plug-in, then that would be the Digital World demo: June 4, 1995.

SS: About a year ago, I think.

KD: Harry outlined the concepts in the spring, roughly.

How did it develop?

BH: Through a lot of careful thinking about what is required to provide multimedia over the Internet. It had to be small, powerful, interactive, and safe. It had to provide the capability to create compelling interactions without damaging the resources (computer system) of the user. Thus, Shockwave arose as a careful set of restrictions on the power of Director together with a great compression strategy. The restrictions were designed to make Director Internet safe and affordable. Harry's contribution or invention was to figure this out.

HC: We developed an architecture for Shockwave and built a team of four software and two QA engineers. Later on, a product marketing person came on board to bring Shockwave to market and the Net. The whole process took about ten months.

JN: Painfully slowly. :-) Originally, there were some really nasty problems with Netscape. They were positioning things wrong on the screen, and the 16-bit version of Netscape was crashing randomly when any plug-in would load. I was down at Netscape one day, trying to convince them that they should fix these things so that we could ship Shockwave. They apparently had more important things to work on, so I told them that I would be willing to work on fixing the bugs if they would give me the source code. So after a couple days of digging through the Netscape source, I fixed a major problem in their cache code, and

also fixed the positioning problems that they were having. I also fixed a few other minor problems over the next few weeks, but I can't remember those off the top of my head. The biggest hurdle to get Netscape and Shockwave working together was getting Netscape to implement support for plug-ins and fix their bugs. Our plug-in is actually not that complicated; in fact, Mike Edmunds and I built an OCX for Microsoft's BlackBird in a single weekend. Granted, it was just a prototype, but having a fairly stable environment to work in made things really easy.

SS: Through lots of hard work and not seeing the sun for weeks at a time.

KD: You mean the technology in the project? The idea of an Internet project was floating around MM before I joined last April. I was hired to work on ITV, and Harry, with one or two others, was to do Internet. Both projects (ITV and Internet) were low-budget investments in technology, which had a good chance of being important. But both were seen as technology presences rather than short-term revenue generators. The Internet explosion took us by surprise—fortunately MM had seen the potential and was poised to jump on it. If instead, ITV had boomed, we would have been able to jump that way also.

Smart management here!

Data Transmission for Shockwave

Currently, data transmission is the factor that is limiting your Shockwave movie size. This is soon going to change. Macromedia and @Home, a company whose mission is to provide high-speed data to homes, workplaces, and schools via a cable modem connection, are teaming up.

"It's all coming together so fast. The ability to see interactive multimedia games, education, and business applications running at high speed on the Internet opens up a wealth of possibilities for the creative community and World Wide Web users," said William Randolph Hearst III, president and CEO of @Home. "Shockwave is going to change the look of the Web much as @Home will change the way people access it."

When this venture is completed, the list of features below will be accessible in Shockwave.

Linked media

Linked media will soon be available in Shockwave. Using linked media will enable you to leave media elements on your local file system and still enable users to access them. Linked media includes QuickTime movies as well.

The Next Wave—Shockwave 2.0

Movie in a window

Movies in a window will also be a possibility in future versions of the plug-in. Currently, movies in a window are not allowed because the running movie has no path reference to its original location and cannot, therefore, find the movie in a window.

The "wait for" Lingo command

This tempo channel command currently is not supported, but it will be working in later versions. The Lingo workaround is simple. Putting this script in the same Score script channel will give you the same effect:

```
on exitframe
        go to the frame
end
on mousedown
        go to the frame + 1
end
```

Bandwidth expansion on the Internet

As the bandwidth of the Internet expands (even beyond that of the cable modems) and home users start accessing the Internet at light-speed, one can only imagine what Shockwave developers are going to come up with. Maybe a full-featured HDTV resolution film with 16 digital audio tracks embedded into your Director Shockwave movie will be possible some day.

Macromedia Developer Profile

Name: Sarah Allen
Title: "i write code"

How did you get involved on the Shockwave team?

I worked with Harry Chesley at Apple a few years ago, and he told me about the project. I thought it was a great idea with perfect timing. Shockwave provided an opportunity for me to combine my networking and multimedia experience and apply them to one product.

What is your greatest contribution to Shockwave?

The Mac player (though I didn't do it alone).

What is the coolest thing about Shockwave?

That so many people have started using it, and related to that, I can really see how people are using the software that I write—it helps inform decision-making, helps us find bugs, and is totally motivating.

What is the "uncoolest thing" about Shockwave?

The Macromedia Wallpaper.

What is the one thing you would change in Shockwave if you had enough time?

How much time do I get? The quickest thing I would add is a background color tag, something slightly longer to display the first frame of the movie as soon as we have it.

What is your favorite Shockwave Easter egg?

What Easter eggs?

What one word (other than "shocking") describes your experience with Shockwave?

Fun!

What one statement typifies your experiences during the Shockwave product cycle?

"Just in time software."

How long have you been at Macromedia?

Since June 1990.

Where were you working before?

Adobe.

What did you do?

Adobe ScreenReady.

One interesting fact about you?

I like to make holograms.

Your greatest accomplishment?

Learning to keep a plant alive—although mine did suffer over the Christmas holidays. They didn't die, and are slowly coming back to health.

What are the longest number of continuous hours you have worked at Macromedia?

16.

The Next Wave—Shockwave 2.0

What is the longest wait you've had for a download?

Not too long. We have a T3 and I won't look at anything over 100K at home. And I feel terribly guilty about all those people at 14.4, like my mom.

How many hours do you surf per day?

0–1 hour per day, a few hours a week.

Chapter 11

Shockwave for FreeHand

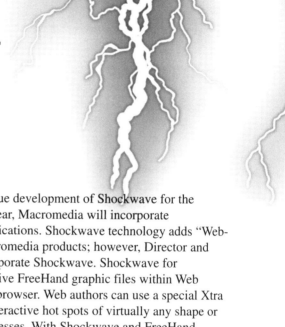

Macromedia has made a commitment to continue development of **Shockwave** for the Internet, and it's likely that by the end of this year, Macromedia will incorporate Shockwave technology into all of its other applications. Shockwave technology adds "Web-ready" capabilities and optimization to all Macromedia products; however, Director and FreeHand were the first of many that will incorporate Shockwave. Shockwave for FreeHand provides the capability to display native FreeHand graphic files within Web pages displayed in the Netscape Navigator 2.0 browser. Web authors can use a special Xtra that has been created for FreeHand to create interactive hot spots of virtually any shape or size, which provide links to different URL addresses. With Shockwave and FreeHand, graphic artists and illustrators can incorporate vector images and designs into their Web pages and have them look just like they did when they were created on their own systems! Shockwave for FreeHand is essentially a new graphic file type that can be incorporated into Web pages (as an alternative to the existing bitmap formats like GIF, JPEG, and so on).

How Is This Related to Shockwave for Director?

Where Shockwave for Director provides the capability to deliver dazzling, interactive multimedia content (with sound, animations, and motion), Shockwave for FreeHand provides the capability to incorporate compact, dynamic, scalable vector graphics into World Wide Web pages. Using this technology, designers can incorporate vector graphics that are true representations that suit the illustrators' desires. A key advantage of vector graphic designs within Web pages is their capability to be scaled or zoomed without compromising the integrity of the image. FreeHand's zoom feature (up to 25,600%) is provided as part of the Shockwave for FreeHand Plug-In. Consequently, users can zoom in very closely to crisply defined details in a geographic map, illustration, or technical drawing. This capability would not be possible at all with current bitmap graphics formats for the Web (such as GIF and JPEG), which do not provide functionality for zooming. Now Web authors can create nicely designed graphics for their Web pages. These can include text on a path, text wrapped around graphics, text in columns, and more.

What Can I Put on the Web with FreeHand?

- With this software, designers can incorporate vector graphics into Web pages that are true representations of the illustrator's artwork.
- Web authors can repurpose vector illustrations that were created in FreeHand, Adobe Illustrator, or CorelDRAW! because FreeHand can easily import files from these other applications.
- Using Shockwave for FreeHand, Web authors can create effects that previously would have required a number of different tools. Consequently, they can cut down on their overall development time.
- With Shockwave for FreeHand, you can design graphics that will download quickly and display crisply in Web pages.
- With Shockwave for FreeHand, Web graphics can now incorporate hot spot links of varying shapes.

Web authors can easily create hot spots of varying shapes and sizes simply by attaching a URL link to vector graphic objects while working in FreeHand. Attaching hot spots is currently a challenge with other Web tools and eliminates the need for image maps for these graphics. For example, a designer could attach links to different states on a map of the U.S. and link to Web pages that provide details of those states. Alternatively, a Web author could attach hot links to different portions of a technical illustration and create links that jump to graphics and show detailed schematics of this piece.

How Does It Work?

Authors can start today, using the current shrink-wrapped version of FreeHand to create their graphics. You can use existing content and FreeHand software (both Macintosh and Windows versions) to produce dynamic artwork for the Net. Macromedia will also provide a special Xtra, which Web authors can use within FreeHand to attach an URL link to FreeHand elements. This is made possible by Macromedia's Open Architecture, which enables many new kinds of Plug-In extensions such as this one.

The browsing process

Users can download the Shockwave for FreeHand Plug-In from Macromedia's Web site and place it into their Netscape Navigator 2.0 Plug-Ins folder. Just like Shockwave for Director, as users browse, FreeHand graphics will load as the page is displayed. Macromedia will provide both the authoring and browsing components free of charge from its Web site (`http://www.macromedia.com`).

Which browsers will support Shockwave for FreeHand?

Macromedia is currently developing a Shockwave for FreeHand Plug-In for Netscape's Navigator version 2.0 for Macintosh and Windows. It is considering support for other third-party browsers that offer an open API.

When Will Shockwave for FreeHand Be Available?

Macromedia is planning to post beta software on its Web site in early February, 1996. Final software release is scheduled for later this quarter for the following platforms:

- The 68K Macintosh
- Power Macintosh
- Windows 3.1 (with Windows 32s extensions)
- Windows 95
- Windows NT (this is a 32-bit application)

Future Applications

With Macromedia's commitment to continue development of Shockwave for the Internet, they are positioning themselves to be the leading software developer of Internet tools.

One of the most exciting tools Macromedia produces is Extreme 3D. Extreme 3D is a spline-based, natural form, 3D modeling, rendering, and animation application. When Extreme 3D supports Shockwave, it's going to enable developers to create amazing 3D objects and then plug those objects into Internet home pages. From within the Internet browser, users will be able to grab and rotate the 3D objects around in real time! A Shockwave version of Extreme 3D, one can only assume, will include the real-time, texture mapping features already found in Extreme 3D. Real-time texture mapping will enable your 3D models to look photo-realistic, yet still enable the user to control spinning and rotation of the objects. This could easily evolve into interactive 3D objects and worlds on the Internet. Imagine a Web page with a 3D rendering of a table. On the table are 3D objects. These 3D objects could be "picked up," rotated, examined, and even played with, all with your mouse. 3D games, where objects have behaviors and real physical attributes such as bounce, run away, or even chase, could all be incorporated into Extreme 3D with Shockwave.

Macromedia has many other applications besides Extreme 3D—all of which will be really exciting to see integrated into the Internet. SoundEdit, for example, could enable real-time streaming of audio across the Net. And as for their other suite of tools, one can only wonder how these will impact the future of the Internet. This kind of technology could result in a paradigm shift in the way people communicate and interact in the world today. Macromedia is truly the company to watch when it comes to the Internet.

Glossary

8-bit graphics: A color or grayscale graphic or movie that has 256 colors or less.

8-bit sound: 8-bit sounds have a dynamic range of 48 dB. Dynamic range is the measure of steps between the volume or amplitude of a sound.

16-bit graphics: A color image or movie that has 65.5 thousand colors.

16-bit sound: Standard CD-quality sound resolution. 16-bit sounds have a total dynamic range of 96 dB.

24-bit graphics: A color image or movie that has 16.7 million colors.

32-bit graphics: A color image or movie that has 16.7 million colors, plus an 8-bit masking or alpha channel.

Afterburner: The post compression application used to decrease the file size of your Director movies.

AIFF (Audio Interchangeable File Format): This type of file is used by audio editing applications to save digital audio data.

Anti-aliasing: A technique for reducing the jagged appearance or aliased bitmapped images, usually by inserting pixels that blend at the boundaries between adjacent colors.

Artifacts: Image imperfections caused by compression.

AVI (Audio-Video Interleaved): Microsoft's file format for desktop video movies.

Bit depth: The number of bits used to represent the color of each pixel in a given movie or still image. Specifically: 2-bits = black and white; 4-bits = 16 colors or grays; 8-bits = 256 colors or grays; 16-bits = 65,536 colors; 24-bits = (approximately) 16 million colors.

Bitmapped graphics: Graphics that are pixel-based, as opposed to object-oriented.

Browser: An application that enables you to access World Wide Web pages. Most browsers provide the capability to view Web pages, copy and print information from Web pages, download files over the Web, and navigate throughout the Web.

Cable modem: Works on the same principal as a normal modem, except that it uses the high bandwidth lines that cable companies provide instead of a phone line (*see MODEM*).

Cache: A hard disk storage area that keeps frequently accessed data or program instructions readily available so that you don't have to retrieve them repeatedly.

Cast member: A placeholder inside Macromedia Director that represents content.

CGI (Common Gateway Interface): A Web standard for the methods that servers and external programs and scripts use to communicate.

Client: A computer that requests information from a network's server.

Compression: Reduction of the amount of data required to re-create an original file, graphic, or movie. Compression is used to reduce the transmission time of media and application files across the Web.

Data streaming: The capability to deliver time-based data as it is requested, much like a VCR, rather than having to download all the information before it can be played.

DCR: File extension for a compressed or afterburned Director movie.

Digital Video: Video that is recorded (captured) on or by a computer.

DIR: File extension for a Director movie.

Disk cache: A (usually) temporary file created by some application used to store data in a place other than RAM.

Dithering: The positioning of different colored pixels within an image that uses a 256 color palette to simulate a color that does not exist in the palette.

DXR: File extension for a protected Director movie.

FTP (File Transfer Protocol): An Internet protocol that enables users to remotely access files on other computers on the Internet.

GIF (Graphical file format): Developed for reading images through the Net.

HTML (HyperText Markup Language): The common language for interchange of HyperText between the World Wide Web client and server. Web pages must be written using HTML.

HTTP (HyperText Transfer Protocol): File type identifier, used to send text and graphical data through the Internet.

ISDN: Consumer level high-speed (128K Baud) Internet connection service provided by your local phone company.

ISP: Internet Service Provider.

Glossary

JPEG (Joint Programmer Experts Group): A graphical file format designed to reduce the size of the graphic as much as 96%.

Lingo: The scripting language used by Macromedia Director to program interactivity into a multimedia presentation.

MIME (Multipurpose Internet Mail Extensions): An Internet standard for transferring file non-text-based data such as sounds, movies, and images.

MODEM (derived from MOdulator DEModulator): A device used to translate digital computer data into audible tones for transmission over a standard RJ-11 phone line. Measured in bits per second, baud, or mega-bits.

PostScript®: A sophisticated page description language used for printing high-quality text and graphics on laser printers and other high-resolution printing devices.

QuickTime™: System software developed by Apple computers for presentation of desktop video.

RAM (Random Access Memory): The temporary (volatile) storage place for running applications.

ROM (Read Only Memory): The permanent storage place for basic computer instructions such as "Look for a hard drive and a file called command.com or system."

SGML (Standard Generalized Markup Language): SGML is an international standard for electronic document exchange and is the basis of the highly popular HTML.

URL (Uniform Resource Locator): The address for a Web site.

Index

Symbols

<EMBED> tag, 85
<NOEMBED> tag, 86
1M download time, 33
2-Lane Media Interactive Advertising and Marketing, 102-112
3D animations, 38
8-bit graphics, 37, 169
8-bit sound, 169
11 Khz sample rate (downsampling), 44
16-bit graphics, 169
16-bit sound, 169
22 Khz sample rate (downsampling), 44
24-bit graphics, 38, 169
30K download time, 33
32-bit graphics, 38, 169
100K download time, 33
200K download time, 33
500K download time, 33

A

advertising, online, 15
Afterburner (post-compression application), 5, 31, 75-79, 169
    compression techniques, 75-79
    name origin, 78-79
    Xtra compressors, 78
AIFF (Audio Interchangeable File Format), 169
Algorithmic Animations in Shockwave, DAVIDEO, 121-127
Allen, Sarah, Programmer, 161-163
animation, 17
    3D animations, 38
    FPS (frames per second), 38
    see also art; graphics; images
anti-aliasing, 169
arcade game reproductions, Saturday!, 152-156
art, effects, adding, 26
artifacts, 169
audio
    8-bit sound, 169
    16-bit sound, 169
    AIFF (Audio Interchangeable File Format), 169
    audio loops, 47-48
    authoring techniques, 44-49
    downsampling, 44-47
    files, cropping, 45
    lead-in and lead-out lag time, 45
    MIME (Multipurpose Internet Mail Extensions), 171
    movies, multiple bytes, 84
    toggling, 48-49
audio loops, 47-48
authoring, 25
    art, 26
    HTML, 84-92
    ideas, 25-33
    Lingo commands, 26
    techniques, 37-55
        audio, 44-49
AVI (Audio-Video Interleaved), 169

B

bandwidth, Internet, expansion, 2, 161
binary raw data, 94
bit depths, 38, 41-42, 169
bitmapped graphics, 169
broken icons, 87-88
browsers, 169
    compatibility, 2, 7-8
    FreeHand, support, 167
    HTML, 87-92
    Netscape 2.0 browser, 31-32
    see also Netscape Navigator 2.0 browser

C

cable modems, 170
caches, 170
cast members, 170
    conservation, 52
    dithering, 40-42
    managing, 49-52
Cast menu commands, Find Cast Members, 52
Cast window, dithering, 40
CGI (Common Gateway Interface), 170
Chesley, Harry, senior architect, 53-55
CL!CK Active Media communications agency, 112-119
clients, 170
Close Window command, 69
CloseResFile command, 69
CloseXLib command, 69
color, cropping unused, 43
ColorDepth command, 65
commands
    Cast menu, Find Cast Members, 52
    Effects menu, Switch Colors, 43
    Lingo, 57-73
        Close Window, 69
        CloseResFile, 69
        CloseXLib, 69
        ColorDepth, 65
        Cursor, 66
        Date, 64
        FileName, 71
        Forecolor Color of Sprite, 67
        GetLatestNetID ( ), 63
        GetNetText (URI), 59
        GetNthFileNameInFolder, 71
        GoToNetMovie (URI), 58-59
        GoToNetPage (URI), 58
        ImportFileInto, 69
        LastEvent, 67-68
        MCI, 71
        MoviePath, 71
        NetAbort, 63
        NetDone ( ), 60
        NetError ( ), 61
        NetLastModDate( ), 62
        NetMime ( ), 62
        NetTextResult ( ), 61
        Open, 70
        Open Window Dcx, 69
        OpenResFile, 69
        OpenXLib, 69
        PathName, 71
        PreLoadNetThing (URI), 59-60
        PrintFrom, 70
        Quit, 71
        Random, 65
        Restart, 71
        SaveMovie, 70
        SearchCurrentFolder, 71
        SearchPath, 71
        Shutdown, 71
        SoundLevel, 65-66
        Tempo Channel, 161
        Time, 64
compression, 170
    Afterburner, 31, 75-79, 169
    current compression technique, 77
    customized compression techniques, 78
    DCR (Director Compressed Resource) files, 31, 170
    future possibilities, 158
    images, artifacts, 169
    movies, 53-55
CompuServe, compatibility, 2
connections
    ISDN connections, 170
    requirements, 33
conservation, cast members, 52
control techniques, movies, 51-52
corporate presentations, 19
cropping
    audio files, 45
    images, 37, 43
current compression technique, 77
Cursor command, 66
customized compression techniques, 78

D

data streaming, 170
data transmission, 160-163
Date command, 64
DAVIDEO multimedia company, 119-127
Day, Ken, Senior Architect, 92
DCR (Director Compressed Resource) files, 31, 95-96, 170
Deep Forest Web Site for SONY Interactive, M/C Interactive, 139-143
digital video, 170
DIR files, 170
Director, 5, 27
disabling
    Lingo commands, 68-73
    XObjects, 68
disk caches, 170
Disney's *Toy Story* concentration game, 21
Disney's *Toy Story* Web site, 9
dithering, 170
    cast members, 40-42
    images, 39-41
download times, 33-35, 83-84
downsampling, 44-47
Dream a Dolphin's New Media Intership Competition, CL!CK Active Media, 114-119
DXR files, 170

E-F

educational training, 23-24
Effects menu commands, Switch Colors, 43
embedding hot points (animated bullets), pages, 26
Extreme 3D, 167-168

FileIO XObject, 68
FileName command, 71
files
    AIFF (Audio Interchangeable File Format), 169
    audio, determining size, 44-47
    AVI (Audio-Video Interleaved), 169
    binary raw data, 94
    compression, 31, 75-79, 170
    DCR (Director Compressed Resource) files, 31, 95-96, 170
    DIR files, 170
    download times, 33-35
    DXR files, 170
    GIF (graphical file format), 170
    JPEG (Joint Programmer Experts Group) files, 171
    size, determining, 34-35
    uploading, 93-96
Find Cast Members command (Cast menu), 52
Fit Model: A Spot Shockwave Experience, 2-Lane Media, 109-112

Index

Forecolor Color of Sprite command, 67
FPS (frames per second), 38
frame window control, future possibilities, 158
FreeHand, 165-167
   browser support, 167
   graphics, creating, 166-167
   WWW capabilities, 166
FTP (File Transfer Protocol), 94, 170

G

games, interactive, 21
GetLatestNetID ( ) Lingo command, 63
GetNetText (URI) Lingo command, 59
GetNthFileNameInFolder command, 71
GIF (Graphical file format), 170
GoToNetMovie (URI) Lingo command, 58-59
GoToNetPage (URI) Lingo command, 58
graphics
   8-bit graphics, 37, 169
   16-bit graphics, 169
   24-bit graphics, 38, 169
   32-bit graphics, 38, 169
   bitmapped graphics, 169
   compression, 170
   FreeHand, creating, 166-167
   ink effects, 50-51
   JPEG (Joint Programmer Experts Group) files, 171
   pixels, dithering, 170
   see also images

H

Hands of Time Animation & Design, 127-136
Hands of Time's Satan Six Pack, 21
hard disks, caches, 170
hardware requirements, 33
Hearst, William Randolph III, 160
high-impact interfaces, 13
hot points (animated bullets), embedding, pages, 26
HTML (HyperText Markup Language), 170
   authoring, 84-92
   broken icons, 87

browsers, 87-92
   Netscape 2.0 browser, 86
   SGML (Standard Generalized Markup Language), 171
   tags
      <EMBED> tag, 85
      <NOEMBED> tag, 86
      TEXTFOCUS argument, 86
HTTP (HyperText Transfer Protocol), 170
   cache files, preloading items, 59-60
   starting and retrieving items, 59
Hunt, Bruce, Director of Networked Players, 72-73

I

images, 37-43
   3D animations, 38
   anti-aliasing, 169
   bit depths, 38
   compression artifacts, 169
   cropping, 37, 43
   index color, 37
   ink effects, 50-51
   pixels
      bit depth, 169
      dithering, 39-41
   see also graphics
ImportFileInto command, 69
index color, images, 37
ink effects, 50-51
installation, Shockwave Plug-In, 28
interactive games, 21
interfaces, high-impact, 13
internationalization, future possibilities, 158
Internet, 2-3, 157
   bandwidth expansion, 2, 161
   connections
      ISDN connections, 170
      requirements, 33
   FTP (File Transfer Protocol), 170
   future possibilities, 157-163
   ISP (Internet Service Provider), 170
   see also WWW (World Wide Web)
Internet Explorer browser, compatibility, 2
ISDN connections, 170
ISP (Internet Service Provider), 170

J-L

Java, Shockwave, compared, 3-5, 76-77
JavaScript, 87-90
   broken icons, eliminating, 87-88
JPEG (Joint Programmer Experts Group) files, 171
LastEvent command, 67-68
lead-in and lead-out lag time, audio files, 45
Lingo scripting language, 26, 57-73, 171
   commands
      Close Window, 69
      CloseResFile, 69
      CloseXLib, 69
      ColorDepth, 65
      Cursor, 66
      Date, 64
      disabling, 68-73
      FileName, 71
      Forecolor Color of Sprite, 67
      GetLatestNetID ( ), 63
      GetNetText (URI), 59
      GetNthFileNameInFolder, 71
      GoToNetMovie (URI), 58-59
      GoToNetPage (URI), 58
      ImportFileInto, 69
      LastEvent, 67-68
      MCI, 71
      MoviePath, 71
      NetAbort, 63
      NetDone ( ), 60
      NetError ( ), 61
      NetLastModDate( ), 62
      NetMime ( ), 62
      NetTextResult ( ), 61
      Open, 70
      Open Window Dcx, 69
      OpenResFile, 69
      OpenXLib, 69
      PathName, 71
      PreLoadNetThing (URI), 59-60
      PrintFrom, 70
      Quit, 71
      Random, 65
      Restart, 71
      SaveMovie, 70
      SearchCurrentFolder, 71
      SearchPath, 71

Shutdown, 71
SoundLevel, 65-66
Tempo Channel, 161
Time, 64
future possibilities, 158
linked media, 160
looping
    audio, 47-48
    movies, 84

M

M/B Interactive, 136-143
Macintosh-based HTTP servers, mime types, setting, 97
Macromedia Director, 27
Macromedia home page, 82
Macromedia Shockwave Gallery Web site, 10
Macromedia Shockwave Plug-In, 5
MCI command, 71
memory
    caches, 170
    disk caches, 170
    RAM (Random Access Memory), 33, 171
    ROM (Read-Only Memory), 171
MIME (Multipurpose Internet Mail Extensions), 96-100, 171
modems, 171
    cable modems, 170
    download times, 33-35
    requirements, 33
monitors, requirements, 33
mono sound files, 44
MoviePath command, 71
movies
    art, re-creating, 26
    audio, authoring techniques, 44-49
    authoring
        ideas, 25-33
        techniques, 37-55
    compression, 53-55, 75-79, 170
    control techniques, 51-52
    Digital Video, 170
    download times, 33-35
    file sizes, determining, 34-35
    hot points (animated bullets), embedding, 26
    Lingo commands, 26
    looping, 84

pages
    adding, 81-84
    multiple, 84
    QuickTime, 171
    retrieving, 58-59
    saving, 53-55
    size considerations, 38
sound
    authoring techniques, 44-49
    multiple, 84
    toggling, 48-49
    starting, 58-59
    windows, 161
multimedia, Web pages, adding to, 81-84

N

NaviSoft browser, compatibility, 2
NetAbort Lingo command, 63
NetDone ( ) Lingo command, 60
NetError ( ) Lingo command, 61
NetLastModDate( ) Lingo command, 62
NetMime ( ) Lingo command, 62
Netscape Communications, alliance, 6-7
Netscape Navigator 2.0 browser, 31-32
    compatibility, 2
    frame window control, future possibilities, 158
    HTML, 86
    movies, viewing, 85-86
NetTextResult ( ) Lingo command, 61
Newlin, John, Developer, 98
NewOrder Media, 143-148
Not Ghost ink effect, 50

O-P

online advertising, 15
Open command, 70
Open Window Dcx command, 69
opening URIs (Uniform Resource Identifiers), 58
OpenResFile command, 69
OpenXLib command, 69
operating systems, compatibility, 4
OrthoPlay XObject, 68

pages
    animations, 17
    download times, 83-84
    files, uploading, 93-96
    hot points (animated bullets), embedding, 26
    movies
        adding, 81-84
        multiple, 84
    site bytes, 17
    size considerations, 83-84
    URLs (Uniform Resource Locators), 171
Paint window, dithering, 40
Panic in the Park for Warner*Active*, 2-Lane Media, 104-109
PathName command, 71
pixels
    bit depth, 169
    dithering, 39-41, 170
platforms, compatibility, 4
Pop Rocket Shockwave Game Arena Web site, 13
Pop Rocket's !FatShooterMan!, 21
PostScript, 171
PPP accounts, 33
PreLoadNetThing (URI) Lingo command, 59-60
presentations, 19
PrintFrom command, 70

Q-R

Quatris (Tetris) arcade game, 153
QuickTime, 171
Quit command, 71

RAM (Random Access Memory), 33, 171
Random command, 65
Restart command, 71
retrieving
    HTTP items, 59
    movies, 58-59
Reverse ink effect, 50
ROM (Read-Only Memory), 171

S

sample rates (audio), 44
Satan Six Pack, 21
Satan's 666 Pack Animations, Hands of Time, 132-136

Index

Saturday!, 149-156
SaveMovie command, 70
saving movies, 53-55
Score window, 42, 49-52
scripting languages
    JavaScript, 89-90
    Lingo scripting language, 171
    PostScript, 171
SearchCurrentFolder command, 71
SearchPath command, 71
SerialPort XObject, 68
servers
    clients, 170
    mime types, setting, 96-100
SGML (Standard Generalized Markup Language), 171
Sheridan, Sherri, Artist/Engineer, 90-92
Shockwave, 1, 9-10
    advancements, 5
    FreeHand, 165-167
    future possibilities, 157-163
    hardware requirements, 33
    history, 158-160
    home page, 82
    Java, compared, 3-5, 76-77
    opportunities, 101-156
    Plug-In, 5, 27
        installing, 28
        troubleshooting, 28-31
    software requirements, 5, 26-32
    uses, 11-24
Shutdown command, 71
site bytes, 17
size
    files, determining, 34-35, 44-47
    pages, considerations, 83-84
SLIP accounts, 33
software
    Afterburner (post-compression application), 31, 75-79
    Extreme 3D, 167-168
    FreeHand, 165-167
    Macromedia Director, 27
    Netscape 2.0 browser, 31-32
    QuickTime, 171
    requirements, 5, 26-32
    Shockwave Plug-In, 27-31
    SoundEdit Pro, 45

sound
    8-bit sound, 169
    16-bit sound, 169
    AIFF (Audio Interchangeable File Format), 169
    audio loops, 47-48
    authoring techniques, 44-49
    downsampling, 44-47
    lead-in and lead-out lag time, 45
    MIME (Multipurpose Internet Mail Extensions), 171
    movies, multiple, 84
    toggling, 48-49
SoundEdit Pro, 45
SoundLevel command, 65-66
Spot Web site, 110
starting
    HTTP items, 59
    movies, 58-59
stereo sound files, 44
'Stroids (Astroids) arcade game, 153-156
Subtract ink effect, 50
Switch Colors command (Effects menu), 43

T

tags
    <EMBED> tag, 85
    <NOEMBED> tag, 86
Tempo Channel command, 161
text, cropping unused, 43
TEXTFOCUS argument, 86
Time command, 64
TIME magazine Web site, 10
toggling sound, movies, 48-49
Tools window, 42
training, 23-24
transitions, ink effects, 51
troubleshooting Shockwave Plug-In, 28-31
tutorials, 23-24

U-Z

UNIX Servers, mime types, setting, 96-97
uploading files, 93-96

URIs (Uniform Resource Identifiers), opening, 58
URLs (Uniform Resource Locators), 171

virtual worlds, 21

Walcott, Chris, QA Developer, 99-100
WebForce browser, compatibility, 2
WebSTAR servers, mime types, setting, 97
windows
    frame window control, future possibilities, 158
    movies, 161
    Score window, 42
    Tools window, 42
Windows NT operating system, future support possibilities, 158
WWW (World Wide Web)
    browsers, 169
    CGI (Common Gateway Interface), 170
    FreeHand, graphics capabilities, 166
    HTML (HyperText Markup Language), 170
    HTTP (HyperText Transfer Protocol), 170
    URLs (Uniform Resource Locators), 171

XObjects
    disabled, 68
    FileIO XObject, 68
    future support possibilities, 158
    OrthoPlay XObject, 68
    SerialPort XObject, 68
Xtra compressors (Afterburner), 78

GET CONNECTED
to the ultimate source of computer information!

The MCP Forum on CompuServe

Go online with the world's leading computer book publisher! Macmillan Computer Publishing offers everything you need for computer success!

Find the books that are right for you!
A complete online catalog, plus sample chapters and tables of contents give you an in-depth look at all our books. The best way to shop or browse!

- ➤ Get fast answers and technical support for MCP books and software
- ➤ Join discussion groups on major computer subjects
- ➤ Interact with our expert authors via e-mail and conferences
- ➤ Download software from our immense library:
  - ▷ Source code from books
  - ▷ Demos of hot software
  - ▷ The best shareware and freeware
  - ▷ Graphics files

Join now and get a free CompuServe Starter Kit!

To receive your free CompuServe Introductory Membership, call **1-800-848-8199** and ask for representative #597.

The Starter Kit includes:
- ➤ Personal ID number and password
- ➤ $15 credit on the system
- ➤ Subscription to *CompuServe Magazine*

Once on the CompuServe System, type:

GO MACMILLAN

for the most computer information anywhere!

WANT MORE INFORMATION?

CHECK OUT THESE RELATED TOPICS OR SEE YOUR LOCAL BOOKSTORE

Adobe Press

Published by Hayden Books, the Adobe Press Library reveals the art and technology of communication. Designed and written by designers for designers, best-selling titles include the Classroom in a Book (CIAB) series for both *Macintosh* and *Windows* (*Adobe Photoshop CIAB, Advanced Adobe Photoshop CIAB, Adobe PageMaker CIAB, Advanced Adobe PageMaker CIAB, Adobe Illustrator CIAB,* and *Adobe Premiere CIAB*), the Professional Studio Techniques series (*Production Essentials, Imaging Essentials, and Design Essentials, 2E*), and *Interactivity by Design.*

Design and Desktop Publishing

Hayden Books is expanding its reach to the design market by publishing its own mix of cutting-edge titles for designers, artists, and desktop publishers. With many more to come, these must-have books include *Designer's Guide to the Internet, Photoshop Type Magic, Adobe Illustrator Creative Techniques, Digital Type Design Guide,* and *The Complete Guide to Trapping, 2E.*

Internet and Communications

By answering the questions of what the Internet is, how you get connected, and how you can use it, *Internet Starter Kit for Macintosh* (now in 3rd ed.) and *Internet Starter Kit for Windows* (now in 2nd ed.) have proven to be Hayden's most successful titles ever, with over 500,000 *Starter Kits* in print. Hayden continues to be in the forefront by meeting your ever- popular demand for more Internet information with additional titles, including *Simply Amazing Internet for Macintosh, Create Your Own Home Page for Macintosh, Publishing on the World Wide Web, World Wide Web Design Guide, World Wide Web Starter Kit, net.speak: The Internet Dictionary,* and *Get on the Internet in 5 Minutes for Windows and Macintosh.*

Multimedia

As you embrace the new technologies shaping multimedia, Hayden Books will be publishing titles that help you understand and create your own multimedia projects. Books written for a wide range of audience levels include *Multimedia Starter Kit for Macintosh, 3-D Starter Kit for Macintosh, QuickTime: The Official Guide for Macintosh Users, Virtual Playhouse, Macromedia Director Design Guide,* and *Macromedia Director Lingo Workshop.*

High-Tech

Hayden Books addresses your need for advanced technology tutorials and references by publishing the most comprehensive and dynamic titles possible, including *Programming Starter Kit for Macintosh, Tricks of the Mac Game Programming Gurus, Power Macintosh Programming Starter Kit, FoxPro Machete: Hacking FoxPro for Macintosh, 2E,* and *The Tao of AppleScript: BMUG's Guide to Macintosh Scripting, 2E.*

Orders/Customer Service **800-763-7438**   Source Code **HAYB**

Hayden Books   201 West 103rd Street ◆ Indianapolis, Indiana 46290 USA

Visit our Web page at http://www.mcp.com/hayden/

REGISTRATION CARD

Macromedia Shockwave for Director

Hayden Books

Name _____ Title _____

Company _____ Type of business _____

Address _____

City/State/ZIP _____

Have you used these types of books before? ☐ yes   ☐ no

If yes, which ones? _____
_____

How many computer books do you purchase each year? ☐ 1–5   ☐ 6 or more

How did you learn about this book? _____

    ☐ recommended by a friend   ☐ received ad in mail
    ☐ recommended by store personnel   ☐ read book review
    ☐ saw in catalog   ☐ saw on bookshelf

Where did you purchase this book? _____

Which applications do you currently use? _____

Which computer magazines do you subscribe to? _____

What trade shows do you attend? _____

Please number the top three factors which most influenced your decision for this book purchase.

    ☐ cover   ☐ price
    ☐ approach to content   ☐ author's reputation
    ☐ logo   ☐ publisher's reputation
    ☐ layout/design   ☐ other _____

Would you like to be placed on our preferred mailing list? ☐ yes   ☐ no   e-mail address _____

☐ **I would like to see my name in print!** You may use my name and quote me in future Hayden products and promotions. My daytime phone number is: _____

Comments _____
_____
_____

Hayden Books   Attn: Product Marketing ◆ 201 West 103rd Street ◆ Indianapolis, Indiana 46290 USA

Fax to **317-581-3576**   Visit our Web Page **http://WWW.MCP.com/hayden/**

Fold Here

BUSINESS REPLY MAIL
FIRST-CLASS MAIL PERMIT NO. 9918 INDIANAPOLIS IN

POSTAGE WILL BE PAID BY THE ADDRESSEE

**NO POSTAGE
NECESSARY
IF MAILED
IN THE
UNITED STATES**

HAYDEN BOOKS
Attn: Product Marketing
201 W 103RD ST
INDIANAPOLIS IN 46290-9058

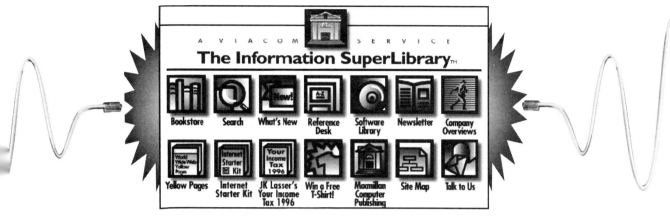

The Macmillan Information SuperLibrary™

Free information and vast computer resources from the world's leading computer book publisher—online!

FIND THE BOOKS THAT ARE RIGHT FOR YOU!

A complete online catalog, plus sample chapters and tables of contents give you an in-depth look at *all* of our books, including hard-to-find titles. It's the best way to find the books you need!

- STAY INFORMED with the latest computer industry news through our online newsletter, press releases, and customized Information SuperLibrary Reports.
- GET FAST ANSWERS to your questions about MCP books and software.
- VISIT our online bookstore for the latest information and editions!
- COMMUNICATE with our expert authors through e-mail and conferences.
- DOWNLOAD SOFTWARE from the immense MCP library:
    - Source code and files from MCP books
    - The best shareware, freeware, and demos
- DISCOVER HOT SPOTS on other parts of the Internet.
- WIN BOOKS in ongoing contests and giveaways!

FTP: ftp.mcp.com

WORLD WIDE WEB: **http://www.SuperLibrary.com**

About the CD-ROM

To access the CD-ROM from the Macintosh, make sure that you have the latest version of the "Apple CD-ROM" system extension installed. This is a hybrid CD; therefore on the Macintosh you will see two folders: one named "MAC" and one named "Win." You should only access the files from the MAC folder if you are on a Macintosh. On a PC the MAC directory is not visible.

The folder named "Macromedia Software" (just "SOFTWARE" on the PC) contains a demo of Authorware, Director, Fontographer, FreeHand and SoundEdit 16. All of these applications need to be installed on your internal hard drive before you can use them.

In the folder named "Tutorial" ("TUTORIAL" on the PC), you will find examples for chapters 2, 4, 5, 7, 8, 9 and other samples.

The folder "RealWorld" ("REALWRLD" on the PC) contains examples from real developers. You can take these apart and see how they were created.

The folder "Macromedia Knowledge Base" ("MM_KB" on the PC) contains the complete technical support database used by Macromedia's technical support department.

Before you call Macromedia with a possible problem, look in the Knowledge base for answers. The "Additional software" folder contains try-out versions of DeBabelizer Lite# LE and Adobe Photoshop #3.0.5. (Sorry, Macintosh only.)